COLORADO

COOK BOOK

Edited by

Drew Garrity

Cooking Across America
Cookbook Collection™

GOLDEN WEST ☼ PUBLISHERS

Printed in the United States of America

11th Printing © 2004

ISBN # 0-914846-67-1

Golden West Publishers, Inc.
4113 N. Longview Ave.
Phoenix, AZ 85014, USA
800-658-5830

For free sample recipes and complete Table of Contents for every Golden West cookbook, visit our website: **goldenwestpublishers.com**

Introduction

Champagne-powder skiing. Hiking among golden groves of aspen. Camping in the columbines. Fishing a Gold Medal trout stream. Rafting roller-coaster rapids. Dancing in Denver. Hunting wildflowers in Crested Butte or wild game in Granby. Mountain biking on Monarch Pass...

Welcome to Colorado... in the 1990s. Each year, millions of visitors make the pilgrimage to the centennial state--to explore its sporting adventures and revel in its regal scenery. And rest assured, there is more than any individual could experience in a lifetime. To visit Colorado present, though, one can't help but visit Colorado past. For even under fluorescent city lights, one will find a historic schoolhouse; even while skiing at a 20th-century glitzy resort, one will cross a century-old trail traipsed by many a weary miner on the road to millions.

Colorado cooking is, likewise, an anomaly: A juxtaposition of new and old, of Southwestern nouveau against cowboy cuisine, miners' rations, hunters' wild game and the Native American's triad of corn, squash and beans. Many of the ingredients remain the same throughout the history, but preparations unfold into another historical dimension... that of Colorado's settlers, who traveled from Spain, Mexico, Italy, France, Ireland, England and Germany to call the Rocky Mountain state their home.

While piecing together the **Colorado Favorites Cookbook**, we've pulled together favorites of days gone and days present, and entwined tales of both. This is by no means a history book... just a sampling of stories that add color to the state's history. Nor is this a recreational guide or travel brochure... although we've brought a bit of both to these pages. Finally, the Colorado Cookbook doesn't promise to be the all-inclusive encyclopedia of the state's cuisine... just a taste to whet the appetite.

In a word, Colorado cooking is a kaleidoscope... of culture, history and life styles. We invite you to enjoy its many colorful dimensions.

Contents

Appetizers

Salads

Soups

The Main Course

Mexican Favorites

On the Side

Breads, Rolls and Muffins

Desserts

Breakfast and Brunch

Beverages

HIGH ALTITUDE COOKING

A simple rule of thumb for cooking at higher altitudes: The higher up, the longer foods need to cook. That's because water has a lower boiling point--approximately nine degrees lower for every 5,000-foot gain in elevation. For example, water boils at 212° Fahrenheit at sea level, but at 203° at 5,000 feet.

For vegetables, plan on adding a bit more liquid and about 7 to 10 percent more cooking time for every 1,000 feet above sea level. Soups will also need to simmer longer; add more liquid as necessary. For meats, no adjustments are necessary for altitudes under 7,000 feet, but cook longer and test meat for doneness at higher elevations. Finally, when baking cakes, reduce baking powder and sugar slightly, and add a bit more liquid. Bake as directed, but do the toothpick test before removing from oven.

Appetizers

In Colorado mountain towns, "happy hour" hits about 4 o'clock in the afternoon. That's just about the time that the day's adventures wind down and local pubs start to swell with clientele. The attire pays tribute to the sports that consume many Coloradans: mountain biking, hiking, rock climbing, fishing, hang gliding, skiing and snow mobiling. The beer taps flow as quickly as spring runoff and the kitchen cranks out dishes heaped high with appetizers. It's a time to share food, drink and grand stories of the day's accomplishments.

Several of the following recipes are inspired by the "happy hour" appetite--the outdoor enthusiast who is as hungry as a horse after a day's play. Paired with a salad, these may pass as an entire meal. Or, plan to serve them as appetizers in the true sense of the word: full-flavored finger foods to warm up the taste buds for courses yet to come.

Mexican foods have long been a favorite in Colorado. Often an abundance of food, they're well suited to feed a ravenous group just returning from a day's outing in the mountains. We'll begin with a couple of old favorites...

A Mountain of Nachos

A mound of chips smothered with veggies, beans and melted cheese.

Tortilla chips 1 large bag
Refried beans 1 can
Jack cheese 1 cup, shredded
Cheddar cheese 1 cup, shredded

Green chiles 1 (4 oz.) can, diced
Onion 3/4 cup, chopped
Green pepper 1/2 cup, diced
Tomatoes 3/4 cup, chopped

Spread half the chips evenly on a baking sheet. Drop teaspoonfuls of refried beans, and sprinkle half the cheese and vegetables (except tomatoes) evenly over the chips. Repeat for a second layer. Bake at 325° until cheese is bubbly. Cover the top with tomatoes and return to the oven for an additional five minutes. Serve with sour cream, guacamole and salsa. Variations: Add cooked ground beef, chicken, turkey, pork and other chopped vegetables to layers before cooking.

Pizza Tortillas

Tortillas 2 large flour
Cheese 1/2 cup, shredded
Green chiles 1/4 cup, diced

Onion 1/4 cup, diced
Jalapenos as desired
Salsa 1/2 cup

Heat tortillas on an oven rack until slightly rigid. Transfer them to a baking sheet. Sprinkle on all ingredients except the salsa. Place under broiler until cheese is bubbly. (To avoid burning tortilla edges, move the pan around a couple of times while broiling.) Allow them to cool for a minute before slicing in wedges like a pizza.

It was a sleepy mining town, and although history still hangs from the eaves of every Victorian home, Crested Butte is now a high-spirited adventurer's paradise of skiing, mountain biking and outdoor recreation.

Crested Butte Quesadillas

Tortillas 4 large flour
Refried beans 1 can
Cheese 1 cup, shredded
Tomatoes 3/4 cup, chopped
Green chiles 1 (4 oz.) can, diced

Jalapenos as desired
Onion 1/2 cup, diced
Lettuce 1 cup, shredded
Salsa 1/2 cup
Sour cream 1/2 cup

Place tortillas on lower rack of broiler and cook just until slightly golden. Remove and transfer two tortillas to baking sheet. Spread refried beans on each and cover with all but 1/3 cup of cheese. Sprinkle on half the tomatoes, and all the green chiles, jalapenos and onion. Bake at 350° until cheese is bubbly, taking care not to burn the tortilla edges. Lightly sprinkle the remaining tortillas with water. Place them on top of the quesadillas and cover with remaining cheese. Bake an additional five minutes. Remove from the oven and allow to cool for a couple of minutes. Garnish quesadillas with lettuce, salsa, sour cream and the remaining tomatoes.

Villa de Ville Chili con Queso

Janice E. James—Kirk, Colorado: "My family likes it spicy hot, but others may prefer hamburger or mild sausage, mild cheese and chiles."

Hot sausage 1/2 pound
Cream of mushroom soup 1 can
Cheese 1/2 pound, extra sharp, shredded
Worcestershire sauce 1 teaspoon

Dry mustard 1 teaspoon
Green chiles 1 (4 oz,) can, diced or, **Jalapeno chiles** 1 (4 oz) can, diced
Salt to taste

Brown sausage in skillet and break it into small pieces. Drain off fat. Place in top of double boiler and add remaining ingredients. Simmer until cheese melts; stir to mix, but **do not overmix**. Pour into chafing dish and serve with chips or vegetables.

Formerly named the White Buttes, the Pawnee Buttes rise 300 feet above the otherwise geographically mundane area near Fort Morgan--an agricultural and ranching center in Northeastern Colorado. The Buttes are rooted in the Pawnee National Grasslands, a comfortable and secluded picnicking spot best visited in spring and fall.

Pawnee Parmesan Chips

Serve with dips, under melted cheese or floating atop a bowl of soup.

Oil for frying
Corn tortillas cut in strips

Parmesan grated
Cayenne and salt to taste

Deep fry tortilla strips until golden; remove with a slotted spoon and allow to drain on paper towel. Sprinkle on parmesan and gently toss. Spread chips on a baking sheet, sprinkle on cayenne as desired. Bake at 225° until cheese melts, about five minutes.

Black Bean Dip

Lee Schillereff—Canon City, Colorado: "This recipe won first prize at the Colorado Springs Dietary Association's low-cal, low-fat contest."

Black beans 1 can, with juice **Vinegar** 1 tablespoon
Garlic 2 cloves **Salt** 1/2 teaspoon

In an electric blender, puree all ingredients together. Serve with tortilla chips or pita bread cut into quarters.

Each spring in Ignacio, Colorado, the Southern Ute Indian Tribe celebrates the end of winter with the Bear Dance and festival. Dressed in traditional costumes--similar to those worn in the 15th century when Spanish explorers in Ute territory first encountered the dance--the Native Americans perform a free-flowing exaggerated dance mimicking bears awakening from hibernation. The public is invited to attend the weekend celebrations and encouraged to give the dance a whirl. The Ute Bear Dance philosophy? "Leave your troubles behind and start your life anew."

Ignacio Green Chile Pinwheels

Virginia E. Payne—Ignacio, Colorado

Tortillas 6 flour **Ham** 1 1/2 pounds, thinly sliced
Cream Cheese 8 ounces **Green chiles** 1 (4 oz.) can,
Green or red chile jelly 1 jar chopped, or 1 cup fresh chiles

Lay tortillas flat and spread cream cheese then jelly to cover evenly. Place a slice of ham on top. Sprinkle on green chiles. Roll tortillas and space toothpicks evenly to hold in place. Cut into bite-size snacks and serve.

Rocky Ford Cantaloupe
and
Sesame Chicken Kabobs

Known as the "agricultural capital of the Arkansas Valley," Rocky Ford is most famous for its cantaloupes. In fact, melons grown here provide seed stock for many of the cantaloupes grown worldwide.

Chicken 5 pounds, boneless breast meat, cut into pieces
Butter 1/2 cup butter
Sesame oil 1 1/2 tablespoons
Soy sauce 1/4 cup
Hot mustard 1 tablespoon

Honey 1 cup
Egg 1 at room temperature
Peanut oil 3/4 cup
Cantaloupes 2 large
Sesame seeds 1 1/2 cups, toasted

Saute chicken in skillet with melted butter, cooking it in small portions and adding more butter as necessary. Set cooked chicken aside on paper towel to blot off excess grease. Blend together for 15 seconds the sesame oil, soy sauce, mustard, honey and egg. Continue blending while pouring in peanut oil. In a plastic storage pan or bowl, arrange chicken and pour sauce over all, stirring to coat well. Marinate for at least two hours in the refrigerator, stirring occasionally. Cut cantaloupe into one-inch cubes. Alternate chicken bites and cantaloupe cubes on a skewer, roll in sesame seeds and refrigerate until ready to serve.

Trout Bites

Colorado's state fish is the Rainbow Trout. Here's a quick way to prepare the day's smaller catch as an appetizer. Let guests nibble on these delicious morsels while the "big catch" finishes baking.

Trout cooked and filleted
Bacon cooked until crisp

Cocktail buns or bread
Tartar Sauce 1 cup

Slice trout and bacon into bite-size pieces. Spread tartar sauce onto each cocktail bun. Top each with a slice of trout and bacon. Keep chilled until ready to serve.

Stuffed Zucchini Cups

Miniature zucchini "baskets" stuffed with festive fillings.

Crab-Swiss Stuffing

Zucchini 3 medium (about 6 inches long)
Crab meat 2 (7 1/2 oz.) cans, drained and flaked
Green onions 3, thinly sliced
Mayonnaise 1 cup

Lemon juice 2 teaspoons
Curry powder 1/2 teaspoon
Swiss cheese 2 cups, grated
Water chestnuts 1 can, sliced and diced
Paprika to garnish

Wash zucchini and slice off ends. Cut into one-inch rounds. Gently scoop out core without piercing the skin. Combine crab, onion, mayonnaise, lemon juice and curry powder. Stir in 1 1/2 cups cheese and water chestnuts. Spoon into zucchini cups. Sprinkle on remaining cheese and paprika. Bake at 400° for 12 minutes.

---

*Cooking is like love.
It should be entered into with abandon or not at all.*
— Harriet Van Horne

Chicken Curry Stuffing

Zucchini 3 medium
Olive oil 1 1/2 tablespoons
Onion 1 small, chopped
Flour 2 1/2 tablespoons
Curry powder 2 tablespoons
Chicken stock 1/4 cup
Sour cream 1 cup

Sugar or honey 1 tablespoon
Carrot 1/4 cup, grated
Salt and pepper as desired
Lemon juice 2 tablespoons
Chicken 2 cups, cooked and shredded

Core and cut zucchini as in first stuffing recipe. Heat oil and saute onion. Add flour and curry; cook one minute. Stir in chicken stock and sour cream. Add remaining ingredients and simmer 10 minutes. Spoon into zucchini cups. Bake at 375° for 12 minutes.

SUPER SIMPLE PORK CHILI

Ready in 20 minutes

1 lb. **Farmland Fresh Ground Pork**
1 (15.5-oz.) can chili beans

1 (14.5-oz.) can diced tomatoes with green chiles
1 pkg. chili seasoning mix

1. Cook ground pork over medium-high heat until moisture has evaporated and meat browns.
2. Stir in remaining ingredients; bring to a boil. Reduce heat and simmer 10 minutes.

Makes 4 servings

SLOPPY JOSÉ SHORTCAKES

1 (16.3-oz.) can refrigerated jumbo biscuits
1 lb. **Farmland Fresh Ground Pork**
1 (16-oz.) jar thick and chunky salsa

1. Prepare biscuits according to package directions.
2. Cook ground pork over medium-high heat until moisture has evaporated.
   Stir in remaining ingredients; heat through.
3. To serve, cut biscuits in half. Spoon pork mixture onto bottom half of biscuits; top with remaining halves.

EASY GROUND PORK LASAGNA

Ready in 1-1/2 hours

1 lb. **Farmland Fresh Ground Pork**
1 (1 lb. 10-oz.) jar pasta sauce
1 (14.5-oz.) can diced tomatoes
1 (15-oz.) container light ricotta cheese

1 egg
1/2 cup grated Parmesan cheese
1 tsp. Italian seasoning
9 oven-ready lasagna noodles

3 cups (12-oz.) shredded mozzarella cheese

1. Heat oven to 350°F. Cook ground pork over medium-high heat until moisture has evaporated and meat browns. Remove from heat; stir in pasta sauce and tomatoes.
2. Combine ricotta cheese, egg, Parmesan cheese and Italian seasoning in small bowl; mix well.
3. Spoon 1 cup meat sauce into bottom of 13x9x2-inch baking dish. Arrange 3 noodles on top of sauce. Top noodles with 1/3 ricotta, 1/3 remaining meat sauce and 1 cup mozzarella cheese. Repeat layers 2 more times.
4. Cover and bake at 350°F. for 45 minutes. Remove cover and bake an additional 15 minutes. Let stand 15 minutes before serving.

Makes 12 servings

Ready in 20 minutes

1/2 cup ketchup
1 tablespoon brown sugar

Makes 4 servings

©2005 Farmland Foods, Inc.

1028606

PEEL HERE

Easy Family Recipes

KEEP REFRIGERATED

NET WT. 16 OZ. (1 LB) 454g

Chili Shopping List: Ground pork, chili beans, tomatoes with green chiles, chili seasoning mix.

Farmland®

Food from the Heartland™

FRESH

GROUND PORK

The Keppy Family - Durant, IA
one of many American Farm Families of Farmland

Salads

Mining led to the settlement of Colorado, but once the boom went bust, ingenuity had to take over. With the introduction of irrigation to the fertile valleys of the South Platte and the Cache la Poudre, settlers took a turn at tilling the land. It paid off: Today, Colorado's cash crops include sugar beets (see Desserts), corn, potatoes, dry beans, lettuce, spinach and cabbage. And in many a backyard--be it city, hill or dale--Coloradans are following in their forefathers footsteps, and growing a few crops of their own... from beans, carrots and cauliflower, to onions, sprouts and zucchini. The possibilities for salads are limited only by the imagination. Basically, if it grows in the garden it has a place in the salad bowl. Within these next few pages, we offer just a few suggestions to grow on...

West-Mex Salad

A Southwestern salad teaming up the four food groups in one bowl..

Cooked beef or chicken 2 cups
Salsa 1 cup
Salt and pepper to taste
Kidney beans 1 cup, cooked

Lettuce 1 head, shredded
Onion 1 cup, chopped
Tomato 1 cup, diced
Cheese 1 cup, shredded
Tortilla chips 1 large bag

Simmer meat and salsa to heat through and add seasonings. Mix in beans. Place lettuce in large bowl and top with onion, tomatoes and cheese. Spoon meat mixture into center. Surround with chips. Garnish with sour cream, guacamole or salsa.

The kiss of sun for pardon,
The song of the birds for mirth—
One is nearer God's heart in a garden
Than anywhere else on earth.
— Dorothy Gurney

Hearthstone Inn
Hot Chicken Salad

Dot Williams, owner of the Hearthstone Inn—Colorado Springs: "The secret to this recipe is to heat it until all of the ingredients are hot, but the celery is still crisp. A version of this recipe was a state fair winner a few years back. Leftover chicken salad makes a great sandwich!"

Chicken 2 cups, cooked and cut in cubes
Celery 2 cups, chopped
Mayonnaise 1 cup
Cheese 1/4 cup, sharp cheddar, shredded

Almonds 1/2 cup, toasted and chopped
Pepper
Onion salt
Seasoning salt
Cayenne pepper (optional)

Mix all ingredients together, using a healthy dash of each of the seasonings. Pour into a lightly greased casserole. If desired, top with crushed potato chips mixed with a little cheddar cheese. Bake at 375° for 15 minutes.

Orange Chicken Salad

Virginia Payne—Ignacio, Colorado

Butter 1 tablespoon
Walnuts 1/2 cups
Cinnamon 1 tablespoon
Thousand Island dressing 1/2 cup
Spinach leaves and/or lettuce 4 cups

Red onion 1 large, thinly sliced
Mandarin orange segments 1 can
Chicken 1 cup, cooked and diced (turkey may be substituted, if desired)

In a small skillet, melt butter. Add walnuts and stir for two minutes. Add cinnamon and stir an additional two minutes. Set aside to cool. In a large bowl, combine remaining salad ingredients. Add walnuts and toss gently before serving.

Rawah Cole Slaw

Guests of Rawah Ranch in northern Colorado, enjoy fishing, hiking, horseback riding and splurging on the outstanding meals. This recipe is the creation of ranch owner, Ardy Kunz.

Butter 2 tablespoons
Sugar 1/2 cup
Cider vinegar 1/4 cup
Salt 1/2 teaspoon

Dry mustard 1 teaspoon
Milk of cream 2 tablespoons
Mayonnaise 1 cup
Cabbage 1 head, shredded

Melt together butter, sugar, cider vinegar, salt, mustard and milk. Remove from heat and whisk in mayonnaise. Chill dressing. When thoroughly chilled, pour over shredded cabbage.

The Story of Silver Heels

As legend has it, there was a beautiful dance-hall girl-- nicknamed "Silver Heels" because of her fancy slippers-- who lived in the rowdy mining town of Buckskin Joe. When a smallpox epidemic spread through town, Silver Heels stayed on at camp to care for the inflicted miners. After she, too, became ill and was left with terrible facial scars, she mysteriously disappeared. Years later, the townsfolk occasionally spotted a veiled woman, believed to be Silver Heels, visiting the graves of smallpox victims. As a tribute to her kindness, it is said that grateful miners named a nearby peak Mount Silverheels.

Soups

A small city in southwestern Colorado, Gunnison is often mentioned on national news as the area recording the lowest temperatures in the country. Nevertheless, long, cold, snowy winters don't slow the locals down... they're too busy downhill and cross-country skiing in the mountains. One secret to warming up after a bout in the freezing temperatures is to savor a hot bowl of soup. This section starts off with six easy and delicious soups prepared by Junelle Pringle, owner and operator of Waunita Hot Springs Ranch, a guest house located in none other than the nation's coldest... Gunnison.

Corn Chowder
Courtesy of Waunita Hot Springs Ranch

Bacon 4 slices
Onion 1 large, thinly sliced
Potatoes 2 cups, raw, diced
Water 2 cups
Salt and pepper to taste

Corn 2 (17 oz.) cans, cream-style
Milk 2 cups
Margarine 1 tablespoon

Fry bacon in kettle. Remove from fat and saute onion in drippings. Add potatoes, water, salt and pepper. Cover and simmer 20 minutes. Add undrained corn and milk. Simmer five minutes. Garnish with crumbled bacon and a dab of margarine.

---

*Said the Mock Turtle, created by Lewis Carroll in
"Alice's Adventure in Wonderland:"
"Soup of the evening, beautiful Soup!"*

Cream of Broccoli
Courtesy of Waunita Hot Springs Ranch

Flour 3 tablespoons
Salad oil 3 tablespoons
Chicken bouillon 3 cubes
Onion 1 medium, chopped
Salt and pepper to taste

Water 3 cups
Broccoli 2 cups, frozen or
  fresh, chopped
Milk or cream 1 cup
Cheese 1 cup, grated (optional)

Saute onion in flour, oil and bouillon cubes. Add salt, pepper, water and broccoli. Cook over low heat until broccoli is tender. Add milk and heat through. Add cheese and stir until melted. Serves 6.

When the first settlers arrived in America, they were so astounded by the abundance of wild turkeys that Benjamin Franklin thought the turkey should be named as the national bird. The wild birds were not foreign to Native Americans, who in their native language called the turkey a "peru".

Turkey Noodle Soup
Courtesy of Waunita Hot Springs Ranch

Margarine 1/2 cup
Celery 1 1/2 cups, chopped
Onion 1 cup, chopped
Turkey broth 10 cups (10 cups
  of water mixed with 8 cubes
  of chicken bouillon may be
  substituted)

Turkey 2 cups, chopped
Seasoned pepper 1 teaspoon
Parsley flakes 1 1/2 tablespoons
Egg noodles 6 ounces, dried
Salt to taste

In soup kettle, melt margarine and saute celery and onion until tender. Add broth, turkey, pepper and parsley. Bring to a boil. Add noodles, cooking about 15 minutes longer or until noodles are tender. Salt to taste. Serves 12-15.

Minestrone Soup
Courtesy of Waunita Hot Springs Ranch

Onions 2 medium, chopped
Garlic 3 cloves, minced
Vegetable oil 4 tablespoons
Bacon 2 slices, chopped
Thyme 1/2 teaspoons
Basil 1/2 teaspoon, dried
Tomatoes 4 medium, chopped
Apple juice 1/2 cup

Water 4 cups
Tomato puree 2 cups
Carrots 1 cup, chopped
Broccoli 1 cup, florets
Pasta 1 cup
Salt and pepper to taste
Parmesan cheese to garnish

Saute onions and garlic in oil. Add bacon and cook for five minutes. Add thyme, basil, tomatoes, apple juice, water and tomato puree. Bring to a boil and simmer for 1 hour. Add carrots, broccoli and pasta, cooking until tender. Salt and pepper to taste. Garnish with a sprinkle of parmesan.

The Papago Indians, nicknamed the "bean people," are credited for producing a large variety of beans, beginning with large, flat, multi-colored beans--believed to be the ancestor of all Southwestern species.

Navy Bean Soup
Courtesy of Waunita Hot Springs Ranch

Navy beans 1 pound
Ham bone 1
Water 2 quarts
Salt and pepper to taste

Onion 1 medium, chopped
Celery 2 ribs, chopped
Carrots 2, chopped
Ham 2 cups, minced

Soak beans overnight. In the morning, drain water and pour beans in a soup kettle. Add 2 quarts of water, ham bone, salt and pepper. Simmer 2-3 hours. Add vegetables and ham, and more water if needed. Simmer until vegetables are tender.

Hearty Bean Soup
Courtesy of Waunita Hot Springs Ranch

Ground beef 1/2 pound, lean
Onion 1 medium, chopped
Tomatoes 14-ounce can, chopped
Beans 15-ounce can, kidney
  or pinto
Corn 8-ounce can, whole-kernel

Tomato sauce 8-ounce can
Chili powder 2 teaspoons
Water 1 1/2 cups
Red pepper sauce dash
Tortilla chips crushed

Brown ground beef with onion. Stir in remaining ingredients except tortilla chips. Simmer for 30 minutes. Garnish with crushed chips. Serves 6-8.

> *Often referred to as the "Indian Triad,"*
> *the three most common foods in Native American cooking*
> *are squash, beans and corn.*

Carneice's Corn Soup
Carneice Brown-White—Denver, Colorado

Pork 1 pound, raw
Cornstarch 1 tablespoon
Sugar 1 tablespoon
Black pepper 1/4 teaspoon
Soy sauce 2 tablespoons
Vegetable oil 2 tablespoons
Onion 3 tablespoons, minced

Garlic salt 1/2 teaspoon
Chicken broth 6 cups
Salt 1 teaspoon
Corn 1 1/2 cups, creamed
Eggs 2, well beaten
Green onions 2, thinly sliced

Carefully trim all fat from pork. Chop the pork and toss with cornstarch, sugar, pepper, soy sauce and one tablespoon oil. Heat the remaining oil in a saucepan and stir fry onions and season with garlic salt. Add the broth and bring to a boil. Add salt, corn and pork mixture. Cover and cook over low heat for 15 minutes. Combine eggs and green onions and stir into soup until set. Serves 6-8.

Chowderado

The East Coast has clams... and the Southwest has spicy chorizo sausage... making this Colorado-style chowder unforgettable.

Chorizo sausage 1 pound
Red potatoes 4 medium
Corn 12 fresh ears
Butter 1/4 cup
Onion 1 large, minced

Salt to taste
Cayenne to taste
Flour 1/4 cup
Chicken stock 6 cups
Cream 3 cups

Fry chorizo over low heat until thoroughly cooked. Drain off grease and set aside. Chop potatoes into small cubes, place in a saucepan of water and cook until tender. Slice corn kernels off ears and set aside. In a soup pot, melt butter and saute onions with salt and cayenne. Sprinkle flour over onions and stir just to mix. When flour turns golden, slowly add 3 cups of chicken stock by half-cupfuls, stirring continuously. In an electric blender, puree cream, corn and half the potatoes. Stir this mixture into the chicken-onion broth. Simmer 15 minutes. Slowly stir in remaining broth, cream, potatoes and corn. Simmer an additional 15 minutes to thicken. Garnish with crumbled chorizo.

Amy's Potato Soup

Amy Connerton—Aspen Colorado: "Good served with whole-wheat rolls. Can also be frozen and reheated later."

Potatoes 6-8 medium, chopped
Onions 2 medium, sliced
Celery 3 stalks, diced
Chicken bouillon 1 cube
Milk 1 quart

Worcestershire sauce
2 tablespoons
Season salt 1 tablespoon
Pepper 1 teaspoon
Thyme 2 tablespoons

In a large soup pot, place potatoes, onions and celery. Add water to completely cover and boil until potatoes are tender. Add bouillon and stir in milk. Add remaining ingredients and simmer 45-60 minutes. For a creamier soup, run half the mixture through a blender and recombine.

Southwestern Summer Soup

Fresh vegetables from the garden and green chiles give old-fashioned vegetable soup an extra zing. Serve with warm tortillas and butter.

Chicken or beef stock 3 quarts
Green chiles 1 small can, diced
Onion 1 large, diced
Carrot 3 medium, chopped
Zucchini 1 large, thinly sliced
Yellow squash 1 medium, thinly sliced
Bell pepper 1 large, diced

Broccoli 2 stalks, chopped
Cauliflower 1/2 cup, flowerets
Cilantro 3 tablespoons, minced
Garlic powder 1 teaspoon
Onion powder 1 teaspoon
Oregano 1/2 teaspoon
Cheddar cheese 1 1/2 cups, shredded

In a large stockpot, combine the stock, chiles and onion. Simmer for 30 minutes. Add remaining ingredients except for cheese and simmer over very low heat for an additional 30 minutes. Garnish with shredded cheese.

Plum Creek Cellars' Gazpacho

Best when made with garden-fresh tomatoes and cucumbers, this chilled soup is a cool start for any summer meal; low-cal, too. The recipe comes from a Denver winery--Plum Creek Cellars.

Tomatoes 1 3/4 pound—fresh, chopped, or 32-ounce can Italian plum tomatoes, undrained and chopped
Green onions 3/4 cup, chopped
Plum Creek Cellars' Chardonnay (or dry white wine) 3/4 cup
Cucumber 1 medium, peeled, seeded and chopped

Garlic 2 cloves, crushed
Red wine vinegar 3 tablespoons
Worcestershire sauce 1 teaspoon
Tabasco 1/2 teaspoons
Bouillon 2 cubes
Beef broth 1 1/2 cups
Pitted black olives 1 can, drained, sliced

In a large bowl, combine all ingredients. Cover and chill 24 hours. Garnish with croutons and chopped chives.

Wild Berry Soup

A basket of freshly picked blackberries or huckleberries, sweetened with honey and simmered to make a unique soup. This recipe is inspired by a traditional Native American soup prepared at summer's end to celebrate the abundance of mountain wild berries.

Huckleberries or blackberries
4 cups, fresh, washed
Water about 5 cups
Honey 1/2 to 3/4 cup

Cornstarch 1/4 cup
Water 1/2 cup
Mint sprigs, for garnish

Place cleaned berries in a large pot and cover with water. Bring to a boil, then simmer for five minutes. Add honey, stirring well. Mix cornstarch in the water until completely dissolved. Slowly add to berries, stirring well. Stir and simmer until thick. Pour into bowls and garnish with fresh sprigs of mint.

Hearthstone Strawberry Soup

Dot Williams—The Hearthstone Inn , Colorado Springs: "Delicious as a pre-dinner soup on a hot summer evening."

Frozen strawberries
10-ounce package
Lime juice 3 ounces
Powdered sugar 1/2 cup
Heavy cream 1/2 cup

Sour cream 1 cup
Salt 1/2 teaspoon
Grenadine 2 ounces (optional)
Fresh strawberries
Mint sprigs

In an electric blender, blend all ingredients until smooth. Chill thoroughly. Garnish with slivered strawberries and a sprig of mint.

An elegant country mansion with 23 antique-furnished rooms, the Hearthstone Inn is an award-winning establishment and longtime favorite resting stop for Colorado Springs' visitors. The inn is cherished for its Victorian charm, view of Pikes Peak, and elegant gourmet breakfasts that are served daily.

The Main Course

The day is done. The sunset casts a pink glow across snow-covered peaks. Skis and mountain bikes rest against shingles, and woodstove smoke rises from rooftops. Into the tiny streets dwarfed by snowbanks, seeps the aromas of dinner hour. In these mountain towns, and across the desert plains, the fare varies from cowboy-style ribs, to hearty venison stews, savory chicken casseroles, tempting trout sautes and Mexican feasts. Like all Colorado cuisine, recipes are as much a blend of history and culture, as they are a melange of meats, vegetables and seasonings...

Red Lion Lamb Chops

Guests at the Red Lion Inn--a wooden, turn-of-the-century lodge in Boulder Canyon--enjoy tableside service indoors in the intimate dining room, or in a more casual setting on the upstairs porch.

Garlic 3 cloves, minced
Spearmint 1/4 cup, chopped
Oregano 1/4 cup
Dijon mustard 1/4 cup
Red wine 1/4 cup
Soy Sauce 1/8 cup

Olive Oil 1 pint
Lamb chops 2-3 per person

MINT JELLY
Red currant jelly 1 cup
Spearmint leaves 1/2 cup

Mix spices and mustard. Whisk in oil slowly to form an emulsion. Add wine and soy sauce. Pour marinade over the lamb and refrigerate 24 hours. Broil until done and serve with mint jelly.

When Union Colony—later named Greeley—was founded in 1870, settlers devised a plan to farm the land and raise enough crops to support their new community. They dug a 10-mile ditch to divert waters from the Cache La Poudre River to enrich soils. Their ambition paid off: today, Weld County is said to feed more cattle and lambs than any other state. And, Greeley earned honors as the birthplace of irrigated agriculture in the United States.

Silverton Smoky Chinese Ribs
with Rhubarb Glaze

Penny Moore—Silverton, Colorado: "There isn't one acre of agricultural land in San Juan County, but we do have a natural, wild crop—rhubarb!" First published in The Silverton Public Library's "International Rhubarb Cookbook," this recipe won a first-place ribbon at a rhubarb festival cooking contest.

Pork Ribs 2 1/2 pounds

MARINADE
Soy sauce 4 tablespoons
Honey 2 tablespoons
Medium-hot salsa 2 tablespoons
Liquid smoke 1 teaspoon
Garlic 1 clove, chopped
Sherry 1 tablespoon
Catsup 1 tablespoon

Sugar 1 tablespoon
GLAZE
Cornstarch 1 tablespoon
Sugar 3 tablespoons
Wine Vinegar 3 tablespoons
Soy Sauce 1 tablespoon
Medium-hot salsa 1 tablespoon
Rhubarb sauce 3/4 cup

Trim excess fat from ribs and marinate overnight, turning occasionally. Bake at 350° in a foil-lined pan turning every 20 minutes for an hour or until ribs are browned and start shrinking away from the bone. Simmer and stir glaze ingredients in a saucepan until thick and translucent. Toss ribs in glaze and reheat in oven.

An early miner reportedly yelled out: "We may not have gold here, but we have silver by the ton." And the mining town was thus named... Silverton. Actually, the town did have gold, as well as silver, lead and copper. And once Indian troubles were resolved and a crude mountain road was built to the nearest town of Durango, settlement followed. It was a popular location for Chinese entrepreneurs, who owned many of the local businesses. Perhaps it was this historical inspiration that led chef Penny Moore to create the recipe above.

Barbecued Spareribs

Marjorie J. Gleason—Pueblo, Colorado. "We enjoy these ribs with a baked potato and tossed green salad."

Spare ribs 3 pounds
Vinegar 1/4 cup
Heinz 57 Steak Sauce® 1/2 cup

Salt 1 1/2 teaspoons
Prepared mustard 2 teaspoons
Water

Place ribs in a shallow pan. Combine vinegar, steak sauce, salt and mustard. Pour half the liquid over the ribs and bake 30 minutes at 350°. Turn and baste with remaining liquid. Bake until tender-- about 1 hour. If pan dries out, add water as needed. Serves 2.

Oven-barbecued Ribs

Cecilia Woods—Glenwood Springs, Colorado: "Goes wonderfully with corn-on-the-cob, a lettuce salad and warm French bread."

Pork spareribs 6 pounds cut
into one-rib portions
Ketchup 1 cup
Molasses 1/2 cup, light
Prepared Mustard 1/2 cup
Cider Vinegar 2 tablespoons

Worcestershire sauce
2 tablespoons
Chili Powder 2 teaspoons
Salt 1 teaspoon
Pepper 1/2 teaspoon
Green onion 1 small, minced

Place ribs in a Dutch oven or saucepan, cover with water and heat until boiling. Reduce heat, cover and simmer 45 minutes, or until fork-tender. Mix ketchup and remaining ingredients in a bowl. Transfer ribs to a broiling pan and rack. Broil six inches from flame for 20 minutes, turning occasionally, until ribs are browned. Brush on sauce for last 10 minutes of broiling. Serves 6. (Note: Instead of broiling, ribs may be baked in sauce for one hour at 350°.)

Indians are not wholly credited with inventing the barbecue method of cooking, however, historians believe that tribes barbecued their meat before the days of Columbus.

Veal Zurich

Courtesy of the Red Lion Inn in Boulder, Colorado.

Veal 1 1/2 pounds, cut in
  julienne strips
Mushrooms 3 cups, quartered
Heavy cream 1 cup

Sherry 1/4 cup
Salt to taste
White ground pepper to taste

Lightly flour veal, then saute in butter. Add mushrooms. Deglaze pan with sherry. Add cream, salt and pepper. Simmer until cream reduces enough to thicken sauce. Serves 4.

> *In March of 1870, a group of 300 men, women and children--known as the German Colonization Society-- arrived in the Wet Mountain Valley of south-central Colorado and settled the town of Colfax.*

Sauerbraten

Bertha K. Judd—Fairplay, Colorado: "Translated to English, this is also known as "German Marinated Beef."'

Beef ribeye or rump roast 3 pounds
White vinegar 2 cups
Water 1 cup
Sugar 1/2 cup
Pickling Spices 2 tablespoons

Onion 1 large, sliced
Salt and pepper
Margarine 2 tablespoons
Gingersnap cookies 12 crushed

Place meat in a glass bowl or enameled pan. (Don't use a metal pan.) Combine vinegar, water, sugar, spices, onion, salt and pepper. Pour over meat to cover completely. Cover and store in cool, not cold, place, for 5 or 6 days, turning meat over each day. Drain meat, saving the marinade and brown in margarine. Strain the marinade and pour half over the browned roast. Boil for 2 to 2 1/2 hours until tender. Stir in gingersnaps to thicken. Serve with noodles or boiled potatoes. Serves 4-6. Note: Deer, elk or antelope can be substituted for the beef.

Slow-baked Beef
in Cranberry Sauce
Lee Schillereff—Canon City, Colorado

Beef boneless chuck eye roast,
2 pounds
Salt and pepper to taste

Parsley for garnish
Cranberry sauce 1 (16 oz.) can,
with whole cranberries

Trim fat from meat. Add salt and pepper, place in a Dutch oven. Cover tightly and bake at 300° for two hours. Pour off juices and strain off grease. Return meat and degreased juice to Dutch oven, cover with cranberry sauce. Cover tightly and bake one hour. Degrease sauce. Serve meat, surrounded by sauce and garnished with parsley. Serves 6.

McGraw Flank Steak
Ruth McGraw, owner of McGraw Ranch —Estes Park, Colorado.

Honey 3 tablespoons
Vinegar 2 tablespoons
Ginger 1 1/2 teaspoons
Soy sauce 1/4 cup

Oil 3/4 cup
Flank steak 1 1/2 pounds,
scored diagonally

Mix honey, vinegar, ginger, soy sauce and oil. Pour over steak and let marinade for 4 to 5 hours. Cook on a hot grill for just a few minutes for rare meat; longer if desired. Cut into strips. Serves 4.

Skillet Steak and Onions
Marjorie J. Gleason—Pueblo, Colorado: "This dish is inspired by a recipe from Uruguay, South America."

Butter or margarine 1/4 pound
Onions 3 cups, finely chopped

Steaks 4 individual, any kind
Salt and pepper to taste

Melt all but 2 tablespoons butter in skillet. Saute onions until limp. Sprinkle on salt and pepper and remove from heat. In a separate pan, melt remaining butter and add steaks. Cook until desired temperature. Spoon sauteed onions over steaks before serving. Serves 4.

Cornish Under Roast

News of the 1849 Colorado gold rush spread far and wide. Not to miss a chance at the riches were the men of Cornwall, England. With them came their wives, as well as Cornish recipes such as this one. (Courtesy of Gilpin County Historical Society, Central City, Colorado.)

Steak 1 pound, good quality

Potatoes raw, cut into large pieces

Onion 1 large, sliced

Salt and pepper to taste

Cut meat into strips, removing excess fat. Dip each piece into seasoned flour and roll up. Arrange rolls in baking dish and cover with sliced onions. Add potatoes, one or two pieces of the fat trimmings, and cover almost completely with water. Cook at 325° for one hour or until desired temperature.

On the table spread the cloth,

Let the knives be sharp and clean,

Pickles get and salad both,

Let them each be fresh and green;

With small beer, and good ale, and wine,

O ye gods! how I shall dine!

English Folk Song

Arapaho Antelope Chops

Antelope chops 6, 3/4-inch thick
Salt and pepper
Cornflakes 1 3/4 cups, crushed
Eggs 2, beaten

Half and half 2 tablespoons
Vegetable oil 3 tablespoons
Butter 2 tablespoons

Trim fat from chops. Season with salt and pepper. Dip into cornflake crumbs, then in eggs beaten with cream, and coat again with cornflakes. Heat oil and butter in skillet. Add chops and brown on both sides. Cover and bake 15 minutes at 325°. Turn chops over and bake another 15 minutes, or until tender.

Arapaho National Forest surrounds the Fraser Valley of Northwest Colorado. The area has been a prized hunting ground for centuries, first for Ute and Arapaho Indian tribes, then the ensuing white settlers. Also surrounding the valley are a dazzling array of 13,000-foot peaks, complete with prized powder skiing. The one drawback--frigid temperatures. Said Fraser's mayor, C. B. Jensen: "We don't have logging and railroading anymore, and Eisenhower doesn't fish here anymore... but, it's colder than hell."

Venison Dijon

Venison 1 pound, thinly sliced
  and pounded thin
Flour 1/2 cup
Green onions 2, minced

White wine 1/3 cup, dry
Heavy cream 2/3 cup
Dijon mustard 2 tablespoons

Dredge venison in the flour, salt and pepper. Melt butter in skillet and sear venison until golden brown, about 2 minutes each side. Transfer to serving dish and keep warm. Add shallots to the skillet's juices and saute three minutes. Add wine and cook until it nearly evaporates. Add cream; bring to a boil for 30 seconds. Remove from heat and stir in Dijon. Spoon sauce over venison.

Zebulon Pike Pot Roast

Marjorie J. Gleason—Pueblo, Colorado

Pot roast 3-4 pounds, elk or deer

Stuffed olives 1 dozen, sliced

Salt pork 1/4 pound, sliced

Onion 1 medium, slices

Butter 3 tablespoons

Canned tomatoes 2 cups

Salt 2 teaspoons

Pepper 1/4 teaspoon

Sugar 1 teaspoon

Using a sharp knife, cut small pockets into the sides of the roast and stuff with olives and small strips of salt pork. Brown onion slices in butter. Remove onions and brown roast in the hot fat. Add tomatoes, salt, pepper, sugar and browned onions. Cover and simmer until meat is tender, about 3 1/2 hours. Thicken juices for gravy by slowly blending in flour or cornstarch. Serves 8.

PIKES PEAK: Past and Present

Under orders of the U.S. Army, 27-year-old Lieutenant Zebulon Pike set out to explore the West with 22 men under his command. In 1806, he led the first expedition to Colorado, taking the course of the Arkansas River. It was on this expedition that Pike first laid eyes on the pinnacle that now bears his name. In vain, he tried to lead his men to the summit, but unprepared to mountaineer through waist-deep snow, the troop descended.

Fifty years later, when gold was discovered in the area, thousands of fortune hunters crossed the country in wagons with the motto "Pikes Peak or Bust" painted boldly on the side.

Despite the gold rush, beauty alone would have brought settlers and visitors to the area. And it does. After visiting Pikes Peak, Harvard professor Katharine Lee Bates was so awed by the scenery she wrote "America the Beautiful."

In more recent years, Pikes Peak has gained notoriety with marathoners. Each August, 500 runners race 7,500 feet to the summit. The race is recognized as one of the most grueling marathons in the country.

Anasazi Elk Stew

Wayne Smith—Nucla, Colorado: "Anasazi beans are sweeter than pinto beans and less likely to cause stomach digestion problems."

Elk meat 1 1/2 pounds, diced
Butter 1 tablespoon
Onion 1 medium, chopped
Green pepper 1 medium, chopped
Chile peppers 3 medium, chopped

Salt 1 teaspoon
Corn cut from 6 cobs
Tomatoes 6 medium, chopped
Anasazi beans 2 cups, precooked

Brown elk meat in butter and add onion, peppers and salt. Stir occasionally until meat is brown and tender, and onion is translucent. Add corn, tomatoes and precooked beans and heat through. Serves 4.

In Navajo, "Anasazi" means "Ancient Ones"--the name given to the prehistoric Native Americans who dwelled in the cliffs of southwestern Colorado from approximately 1 to 1300 A.D. The Anasazi gathered wild plants, and grew corn and squash--leading historians to believe they were the country's first farmers. The tribe abandoned the area, for reasons that remain a mystery. Left behind were the spectacular cliff dwellings and mesa-top villages preserved at Mesa Verde National Park.

Venison Roll-ups

Marjorie J. Gleason—Pueblo, Colorado

Round steak 2 pounds, elk or deer
Salt and pepper to taste
Pork sausage 1/2 pound

Carrots 4 medium, quartered
Flour as needed
Shortening 2 tablespoons

Pound steaks thin and cut into 4-inch squares. Sprinkle with salt and pepper. Place sausage on each square. Scrape carrots and quarter lengthwise. Place several strips on each piece of meat. Roll each square and fasten with string or toothpicks. Flour lightly and brown in hot shortening. Place in a baking pan and partly cover with water. Bake, covered, at 350° for 1 1/2 to 2 hours. Serves 6.

Mexi-Colo Corn Dish

Marjorie J. Gleason—Pueblo, Colorado

Elk or deer 1 1/2 cups, cooked and diced
Butter 3 tablespoons
Green pepper 1/8 cup, chopped
Onion 1/4 cup, chopped

Corn 2 cups, whole kernel
Tomato juice 2 cups
Chili powder 3/4 teaspoon
Salt 1 3/4 teaspoon

Brown meat in fat. Add green pepper and onion, and saute until onion is translucent. Add corn, tomato juice, chili powder and salt. Cover and simmer 30 minutes. Serve over brown rice. Serves 6.

*I live not in myself, but I become
portion of that around me;
and to me high mountains are a feeling,
but the hum of human cities torture.*

— Lord Byron

Pan-fried Deer Steak

Carolyn Cotton—Brighton, Colorado

Deer 4 steaks
Flour 3 cups
Garlic Powder 1/2 teaspoon
Salt 1/2 teaspoon

Pepper 1/8 teaspoon
Egg 1, beaten
Milk 1/2 cup

Dredge steaks in flour mixed with garlic, salt and pepper. Pound each steak thin. Beat egg and milk with a fork or whisk. Dip steaks into flour again, then into egg mixture and back into flour. Pan fry in oil or shortening until well browned. Serves 4.

Caribou Steak
with Forest Mushrooms

Set in the mountains outside of Boulder, the historic Red Lion Inn serves its house specialties of wild game, ranging from elk to quail. Also on the menu are fresh fish, lamb and prime cuts of Rocky Mountain beef. The inn was built in the 1870s and retains its rustic, comfortable atmosphere under the present ownership of Chris and Heidi Mueller, who have submitted this exotic recipe...

Shitake mushrooms 2 cups, stemmed and sliced
Tree oysters 2 cups, torn or sliced
Butter 2 tablespoons

Sherry 2 ounces
Stock 2 cups, veal or beef
Salt to taste
Ground white pepper to taste
Elk or caribou 4 steaks

Saute mushrooms and tree oysters in butter. Deglaze with sherry. Add stock, salt and pepper. Simmer 10 minutes, thicken, if desired. Broil or panfry steaks. Add sauce to steaks. Serves 4.

South Park Meatballs

South Park was a favorite hunting ground for Indians, who were attracted by the abundant herds of deer, elk, antelope and buffalo.

Venison burger 1 1/2 pounds
Ground pork 1/4 pound
Bread crumbs 3/4 cup
Garlic powder 1 teaspoon
Onion powder 1 teaspoon
Onion 1 small, minced
Chili powder 1 tablespoon

Cayenne pepper a pinch
Green chiles 1 (4 oz.) can, diced
Milk 1/2 cup
Parmesan cheese 1/4 cup, grated
Egg 1, beaten
Oil 2-3 tablespoons

Mix together all ingredients, except oil. Shape into small meatballs. Heat oil in a large skillet. Add meatballs, cooking slowly until evenly brown. These can be served as an appetizer, a side dish, or tossed into spaghetti sauce and simmered for 45 minutes.

The Puebloan Sandwich

Randy Jelinski—Pueblo, Colorado: "Serve these sandwiches with a few hot peppers and French fries or coleslaw."

Green pepper 1/2 cup, diced
Onion 1/2 cup, chopped
Tomatoes 1 medium, chopped
Mushrooms 1/2 pound, sliced
Garlic powder 1/4 teaspoon

Beef 1 pound, any kind, sliced
Margarine 3 tablespoons
Sourdough bread 8 slices
Mozzarella cheese 8 slices

Saute green pepper, onions, tomatoes, mushrooms, garlic powder and beef in half the margarine. Spread margarine on bread slices and place two slices of cheese on four of them. Grill bread until cheese melts. Pile beef-vegetable mixture onto cheese slices. Cover with the remaining four grilled bread slices. Makes 4 sandwiches.

> *Great things are done when men and mountains meet.*
> *This is not done by jostling in the street.*
> *— William Blake*

BBQ Dinner on a Bun

Maxine Barnes—Lakewood, Colorado: "This is a good low-fat recipe."

Ground beef 1 pound, browned
Onion 1 small, chopped
Green pepper 1 small chopped
Celery 2 stalks, chopped
Tomato sauce 1 cup
Water 1 cup
Bread 2 slices, crumbled

Sugar 1 tablespoon
Vinegar 1 tablespoon
Dry mustard 1 teaspoon
Pepper 1/2 teaspoon
Salt 1/2 teaspoon
Ketchup 1/4 cup
Garlic salt 1/2 teaspoon

Drain grease from cooked meat and add vegetables to pan. Stir in tomato sauce and water. Add remaining ingredients, mixing well. Simmer for 30 minutes. Spoon onto toasted buns. Serves 6.

Lamar Chiliburgers

Ethel Montgomery—Lamar, Colorado: "Turkey is a healthier alternative to beef in this recipe. Add the vegetables, and this is a one-dish meal."

Ground beef or turkey 1 pound
Pinto beans 1-2 ounces, cooked
Hamburger buns 4

Cheese (optional)
Tomato, onion, lettuce, pickles

Brown meat and drain grease. Mash pinto beans and mix with meat. Simmer a few minutes then spoon onto buns. Add cheese slices and chopped vegetables. For open-faced sandwiches, cover buns with beef, beans and cheese and broil until cheese melts.

> *Early developers named Lamar after the secretary of the interior under President Grover Cleveland, hoping he'd feel honored enough to build the area land office there. The plan worked: Lamar was officially established in 1897.*
>
> *Revered as the "Goose Hunting Capital of the Nation," the town is the destination of hundreds of hunters, who congregate there each fall to determine whether or not Lamar's reputation for geese is fair... or fowl.*

Lamb Chiliburgers

Marjorie J. Gleason—Pueblo, Colorado

Butter 2 tablespoons
Ground lamb 1 pound
Green pepper 1/2 cup, chopped
Onion 1 medium, chopped
Pinto beans 2 cups, cooked

Vegetable juice cocktail 2 cups
Flour 2 tablespoons
Chili powder 1/4 teaspoon
Salt and pepper to taste
Hamburger buns 4, toasted

Melt butter; add lamb, pepper and onion. Cook over low heat until browned. Add beans and 1-1/2 cups of vegetable juice. Heat to boiling, then simmer 30 minutes. Mix remaining juice with flour. Stir gradually into meat mixture. Cook over low heat until thickened. Add chili powder, salt and pepper. Mix well. Serve over buns.

Loveland Stuffed Peppers
Diane M. Boone—Loveland, Colorado

Ground beef 1 1/2 pounds
Onion 1 medium, chopped
Salt and pepper
  garlic powder, basil and paprika
Canned tomatoes 28-ounces,
  whole, peeled
White rice 1 cup
Bell Peppers 8, seeded and halved

SAUCE:
Tomato sauce 1 (15 oz.)
  and 1 (8 oz.) can
Garlic powder
Oregano
Basil

Grated Romano cheese
Shredded mozzarella

Brown beef and onion. Add to taste: salt, pepper, garlic, basil and paprika. Add tomatoes with juice. Simmer 45 minutes, chopping tomatoes as they cook. Add rice, cover and simmer until tender. Stir in water in small amounts. In saucepan, mix sauce with spices and heat through. Spoon a small amount of sauce into greased 9 x 13 baking dish. Fill each pepper with rice mixture and place in an oven-proof dish. Top with two tablespoons sauce. Sprinkle on cheeses. Add two tablespoons of water to pan. Cover and bake at 350° for 1 hour. Serves 8.

Neva's Saturday Night Special
Christine Posik—Woodland Park, Colorado

Hamburger meat 1 pound
Worcestershire sauce 1 tablespoon
Seasoned salt 1/2 teaspoon
Pork and beans 1 (16 oz.) can

Tomatoes 1 (16 oz.) can
Bacon 1/4 pound
Brown sugar 1/2 cup, packed

Brown meat and drain off fat. Add Worcestershire sauce and seasoned salt. Spoon mixture into bottom of nine-inch pan. Mix beans and tomatoes and place on top of meat. Lay bacon strips over bean mixture and sprinkle on sugar. Bake at 350° for 45 minutes. Serves 4 - 6.

Colorado Fried Chicken

Marjorie J. Gleason—Pueblo, Colorado.

Egg yolks 2
Corn meal 1 cup
Salt and pepper to taste
Cheddar cheese 1 cup, grated

Egg whites 2, beaten
Chicken 2 (3 lb.) fryers, cut up
Oil 3/4 cup

Mix yolks, corn meal, salt, pepper and cheese. Fold in beaten egg whites. Dip chicken pieces into mixture and then fry in hot oil until golden and tender. Serves 8.

> *Maybe its the long winters and a touch of cabin fever that's responsible, but whatever the reasoning, some Coloradans have gone a little quirky when it comes to festivals. Take for example the Annual Burro Days in Fairplay, where locals stage a burro and llama race in late July. Earlier in that same month, Montrose has been known to host a Ducky Derby, setting a flotilla of rubber ducks loose on the Uncompahgre River. And, if that doesn't seem strange enough, there's always the Heeney Tick Festival, highlighted by the crowning of the Tick Festival King and Queen. Finally, to top it off, Empire kicks off summer with the annual Frog Rodeo and a judging for the prettiest, ugliest, biggest and best-dressed frog.*

Loveland Baked Chicken

Diane M. Boone—Loveland, Colorado

Chicken 2 breasts, boneless and skinless
Salt and pepper to taste
Garlic powder to taste

Rosemary to taste
Cream of chicken soup 1 can
Water 1/2 can

Place chicken in casserole dish and season with salt, pepper, garlic and rosemary. Mix together soup and water, pour over chicken and bake (covered) for two hours at 350°.

Raspberry Chicken

Courtesy of the Prospector Restaurant—Leadville, Colorado. "Bill and Sara Charvat, owners of the Prospector Restaurant, pick fresh mountain raspberries to make this recipe in August and September--when autumn color is at its height in Leadville."

Chicken 2 (6-8 oz.) breasts   **Raspberries** 1/2 cup, fresh
Flour 2 tablespoons   **Raspberry Liqueur** 1/4 cup
Butter 6 tablespoons

    Lightly dust chicken with flour. Saute both sides in four tablespoons butter until golden. Remove to warm plates. Pour raspberries into skillet with chicken drippings and saute one minute. Carefully add liqueur and allow to flame. Add remaining butter to thicken. Pour sauce over chicken before serving.

The Tragedy of Horace Tabor

The story of Horace Tabor, founder of Leadville, has all the makings of a Greek tragedy. Formerly a Vermont stonecutter, Tabor left his home state with his wife to gamble for riches in Colorado mining. He succeeded in his dream when, after buying a seemingly worthless mine, it was discovered the Leadville shafts were home to the famous Chrysolite lode. Up sprang saloons, gambling halls, brothels and theaters; Leadville was in its heyday. Tabor, who had earned a reputation for living in the fast lane, divorced his wife to marry a flamboyant divorcee--Elizabeth "Baby Doe" McCourt. Things took a turn, however, when Leadville went from boom to bust. Tabor died in Denver--penniless. His wife died 36 years later, after freezing to death in a cabin above Leadville. And as fate would have it, his former wife was the only one of the love triangle to die a millionaire.

Chicken La Phan
Jan Catlow—Hot Sulphur Springs, Colorado

Celery 2 cups, chopped
Onion 1 medium, diced
Butter 2 tablespoons
Rice 2 cups, cooked

Apples 2, chopped
Salt and pepper to taste
Sage 1 tablespoon
Chicken 2 fryers, cut in pieces

Saute celery and onions in butter until tender. Mix with rice. Add seasonings and apples. Arrange chicken in baking dish and dot with butter. Cover with rice. Bake for one hour and 15 minutes at 350°.

Back in the mining days of the mid- to late-1800s many a small Colorado town was settled in a wink and deserted in a nod. One such town, Bonanza, became home to 5,000 people, 36 whiskey-happy saloons and seven dance halls. When mining dwindled, so did Bonanza. Reported the <u>Denver Post</u>: "...even the chipmunks left." In 1980, Bonanza ranked as the second smallest town in the state.

Bonanza Bourbon Chicken

Chicken 2 broilers, quartered
Butter 1/4 pound
Green onions 4, chopped
Onions 1 1/2 cups, chopped

Flour 2 tablespoons
Heavy cream 1 pint
Curry powder 1 1/2 teaspoons
Bourbon 2/3 cup

Cook chicken, skin side down, in butter and onions for 20 minutes Flip it and cook 10 more minutes. Transfer chicken to serving dish. Slowly add flour to pan drippings and cook two minutes, watching carefully not to burn. Add cream, curry powder and bourbon. Season with salt and pepper, and cook five minutes, until thick. Pour over chicken.

Chatfield Chicken

Makes for great leftovers that can be packed in a picnic basket or backpack for a day's outing.

Chicken breasts 6 boneless
Salad dressing Italian or Caesar
Bread crumbs 3/4 cup

Parmesan cheese 3/4 cup
Salt and pepper to taste
Parsley 1/4 cup, minced

Moisten chicken breasts in bowl of salad dressing. In another bowl combine the remaining ingredients, mixing thoroughly. Coat breasts in this mixture. Bake at 350° for 40 minutes. Pour remaining salad dressing on chicken before serving.

One of the blessings of Denver is its accessibility to several spectacular parks. Chatfield State Recreation Area along the South Platte River beckons boaters, swimmers, fishermen and windsurfers. In the surrounding foothills, Denverites scramble on foot, horseback and mountain bikes. Twenty miles northeast of Denver, a nine-mile trail encircles Barr Lake--another haven for watersports and picnicking. And there's always Red Rocks Park--best known for summer concerts, but tempting as well for picnickers, who can soak in the sun, scenery and a rock show, all on a summer's day.

Red Rocks Picnic Chicken

This chicken is quick to prepare and quick-to-please any picnicker.

Chicken thighs, breasts, wings or drumsticks

Cayenne pepper sauce
Salad dressing

Broil, bake or deep fry chicken parts until done. Pat off excess grease and allow to cool. Store in a plastic container until ready to serve. To serve: Coat in pepper sauce and toss. Serve with bowl of salad dressing (ranch or blue cheese) for dipping.

Waunita Ranch Chicken

This recipe is excerpted from "Ranch Recipes," written by Junelle Pringle, owner of Waunita Hot Springs Ranch in Gunnison.

Chicken 4 cups, cooked and cubed
Green pepper 1 medium, chopped
Onion 1/2 medium, diced
Celery 2 ribs, diced
Almonds 2/3 cup, toasted and sliced

Sour cream 1 cup
Cream of mushroom soup 1 can
Butter 1/3 cup, melted
Ritz® crackers 1 1/2 cups, crushed
Poppy seeds or paprika

Mix first 7 ingredients and pour into buttered casserole. Top with crushed crackers. Pour melted butter over crackers and sprinkle with poppy seeds. Bake at 350° for 30 minutes. Serves 6.

Three generations of the Pringle family have welcomed guests to Waunita Hot Springs Ranch, a vacation retreat near the Continental divide. In addition to the excellent food, guests get their fill on scenic trail rides, fishing, hiking, hayrides and soaking in natural hot springs.

Mexican Chicken

Onion 1 medium, chopped
Margarine 1/3 cup
Cream of mushroom soup 1 can
Cream of chicken soup 1 can
Evaporated milk 1 can

Green chiles 8-ounce can, diced
Cheese 1 2/3 cup, shredded
Chicken 4 cups, cooked, diced
Tortilla chips 1 bag

Saute onion in margarine. Add soups, milk and chiles to make sauce. Spread chips, rice or flour tortillas in a greased casserole dish. Top with diced chicken, sauce and cheese. Ingredients may be layered if desired. Bake at 300° for an hour.

Colorado Creole Chicken

Chicken 2 pounds, boneless, cut
into pieces and browned
Tomatoes 5 large, chopped
Onion 1 large, chopped

Green pepper 1/2 cup, minced
Celery 1/2 cup, minced
Jalapeno pepper 1/4 cup, minced
Cayenne pepper dash

Stew tomatoes, onion, pepper, celery and jalapeno in small amount of oil, until tender. Add chicken, 1/2 cup water and dash of cayenne. Cover and simmer 30 minutes. Serve with rice.

The bayous and Bourbon Street may be thousands of miles away, but Coloradans don't miss a beat with summer jazz festivals scheduled across the state. There's the Genuine Jazz in July festival in Breckenridge, the Annual Winter Park Jazz Festival, and the Telluride Jazz Celebration... to name a few. To really get in the spirit at these outdoor concerts, we suggest packing along a picnic of Colorado Creole Chicken (above) or the following recipe...

Jazzin' Jambalaya

Chicken 1 fryer, cut up
Butter 1/3 cup
Onion 1/2 cup
Tomatoes 2/3 cup, chopped
Green pepper 1, diced
Celery 1/2 cup

Rice 1 1/4 cups
Jalapenos 1/4 cup, diced
Bay leaf 1
Thyme 1/4 teaspoon
Parsley 1/3 cup, chopped
Cayenne dash

Saute chicken in butter and remove from pan. Saute onion and tomato in the chicken drippings. Stir in green pepper, celery and rice. Stir in chicken and cover with boiling water. Add jalapenos and seasonings; simmer until chicken is tender and rice is done. If desired, stir in 1/2 pound of diced ham. Bake at 350° for 10 minutes.

Southwest Chicken Kiev

Chicken breasts 6 boneless
Green chiles 1 (7 oz.) can, diced
Jack cheese 1/4 cup
Cheddar cheese 1/4 cup
Chili powder 2 teaspoons
Cayenne pepper dash

Parmesan cheese 1/3 cup
Garlic powder 1/2 teaspoon
Cilantro 3 tablespoons, minced
Pepper 1/2 teaspoon
Bread crumbs 2/3 cup
Butter 2/3 cup, melted

Pound chicken till one-half inch thick and place a tablespoon of chiles on each piece. Shred cheeses and mix together. Top each chicken piece with 1-2 tablespoons of cheese. Combine together all remaining ingredients except butter and set aside. Roll each piece of chicken around filling, tucking ends under. Dip each piece in melted butter, roll in bread crumb mixture. Place seamside down in baking dish. Drizzle leftover butter over all, cover and refrigerate at least four hours. Leave covered and bake at 350° for 15 minutes.

> *If I didn't start painting, I would have raised chickens.*
> *— Grandma Moses*

Sweet Sherry Chicken

Chicken breasts 6, boneless
Soy Sauce 4 tablespoons
Ginger 1/4 teaspoon
Duck Sauce 1 jar
Orange juice 1 small can, concentrate

Brown Sugar 1/2 package
Sherry 1/2 cup
Salt and pepper to taste
Lemon slices to garnish
Parsley sprigs

Coat chicken in mixture of remaining ingredients. Bake at 300° for 45 minutes or until chicken is tender. Garnish with lemon and parsley. Spoon over rice.

Fresh Trout Amaretto

This luscious dish is prepared at the Prospector Restaurant in Leadville, Colorado. Leadville is also home to a national fish hatchery, at the base of Mt. Massive--a breathtaking and stunningly beautiful area.

Trout 2 fresh, 10 ounces each
Flour 2 tablespoons
Butter 4 tablespoons

Almonds 1/2 cup, slices
Butter 2 tablespoons
Amaretto 1/3 cup

Lightly dust trout with flour. Melt butter and saute trout, meat side down until golden--about two minutes. Flip fish, add almonds and cook two minutes. Remove fish and slowly add amaretto. If the amaretto doesn't automatically ignite, light it with a match and let it burn for five seconds. If flame continues, cover to smother. Add 2 tablespoons butter to sauce and heat until thick. Serve over fish.

Just east of Gunnison each May, anglers go head-to-head casting lines in the Blue Mesa Fishing Tournament. The team catching the most trout takes home $5,000 and, quite possibly, dinner for the neighborhood.

Tarryall Trout

Tarryall Reservoir, in central Colorado, feeds Tarryall Creek, designated as Wild Trout water for its overload of lunkers.

Trout fillets 2 pounds
Lemon juice 1/4 cup
White wine 1/3 cup
Milk 1/3 cup
Mayonnaise 3/4 cup

Tarragon 3/4 teaspoon
Dill 1 teaspoon
Parsley 1 teaspoon
Lemon 1, thinly sliced

Place fillets in shallow baking pan and sprinkle with lemon juice and wine. Refrigerate at least an hour. Add milk to cover bottom of pan. Spread mayonnaise thickly on fillets and sprinkle each with herbs. Bake at 350° for 35 minutes or until fish flakes with a fork. Garnish with lemon slices. Serves 6.

Velma's Trout Fillets

Betty Light—Gunnison, Colorado: "Velma was an ardent fisherwoman who lived along the Taylor River, a prime fishing stream in the Gunnison country. She was also a fine cook and gave me the idea to add beer to the batter."

Trout 6 medium fillets, skinned
Flour 1 cup
Beer 1 cup
Salt 1 teaspoon

Pepper 1/2 teaspoon
Paprika 1 tablespoon
Lemon
Tartar sauce

Dip fillets in flour and then batter made from thoroughly mixing the remaining ingredients. Fry in hot oil, browning on each side. Garnish with lemon and dollop of tartar sauce.

Angling is somewhat like poetry, men are to be born so.
— Izaak Walton, from "The Compleat Angler"

Trout with Seafood Stuffing

Seafood lovers will think they've died and gone to heaven. This dish graces the menu of the Prospector Inn, a favorite Leadville restaurant.

Bread crumbs 2 cups
Onion 1/4 cup, chopped
Garlic 1 clove, minced
Pimento 1/4 cup, chopped
Italian dressing 1 cup
Whipping Cream 1 cup

Shrimp 1 cup, peeled
Parmesan cheese 1/2 cup
Trout 4 fresh, 10 ounces each
Flour 4 tablespoons
Butter 8 tablespoons
Whipping cream 2-3 cups

Mix first six ingredients together to make stuffing. It should be moist enough to hold together. Add more cream if necessary. Add shrimp and parmesan cheese. Shape stuffing into egg-size balls. Heat butter in skillet. Lightly dust trout inside and out with flour. Saute trout about two minutes on each side. Stuff each with an "egg" of stuffing and fold fish over. Cover with 1/2 to 3/4 cup of whipping cream. Bake at 350° for 10-15 minutes.

Black Mountain Tasty Trout

Simple to prepare; elegant to the palate. This recipe was originally published in the Colorado Dude and Guest Ranch Association's cookbook, "Favorite Ranch Recipes." Tasty Trout was first prepared at Black Mountain Ranch Resort in McCoy, Colorado.

Trout 4, cleaned
Walnuts 1/2 cup, chopped
Bread crumbs 1 cup, seasoned

Butter 1/2 cup, melted
Lemon juice from 1 lemon
Parsley to garnish

Stuff trout with a mixture of walnuts and bread crumbs. Mix melted butter and lemon juice, then brush on fish. Bake at 350° for 15-20 minutes, basting frequently. Garnish with parsley. Serves 4.

Dillon Beer-batter Trout

Beer 1 (12 oz.) can
Flour 1 1/2 cups
Corn meal 1/4 cup
Garlic powder 1 teaspoon
Paprika 2 teaspoons
Salt 1/2 teaspoon

White pepper 1/2 teaspoon
Trout 12 fillets from 6 fish, boned and cut in half
Oil for deep-frying
Parsley to garnish
Lemon 1, cut in wedges

Mix first seven ingredients in a bowl. Dip each trout fillet in batter and fry in hot oil. Cook until golden brown on each side, about eight minutes. Garnish with parsley and wedges of lemon.

Four- and five-pound rainbow trout are not unknown to the waters of Summit County's Dillon Reservoir, which is also stocked with kokanee salmon and cutthroat and brown trout. The county is probably better known, though, for it's famous ski resorts: Arapahoe Basin, Breckenridge and Keystone, not to mention the unlimited possibilities for cross-country and backcountry skiing.

Rainbow Falls Barbecued Trout

Christine Posik—Woodland Park, Colorado: "A freshly caught trout is much tastier than a fish-market trout."

Trout about 2 pounds, or a number of smaller ones
Butter 1/2 cup, melted

Lemon juice 1 tablespoon
Garlic salt 1/2 teaspoon
Pepper 1/4 teaspoon

Clean the trout, leaving on head and tail. Brush generously with basting butter (the remaining ingredients combined) inside and out. Place on oiled grill over medium-hot fire. Baste every three minutes and when turning fish. Fish is done when skin begins to crack. For an extra treat, dip each forkful of fish in melted butter.

Not only is General Palmer in the history books as the founder of Colorado Springs, he is also noted for establishing the first fish hatchery in Colorado. Curiosity seekers may tour the 1871 hatchery while visiting Rainbow Falls Park, near the town of Woodland Park. Other park activities: horseback riding, camping, hiking and feasting on chuckwagon dinners. With 25 acres of lakes brimming with all kinds of trout, Rainbow Falls Park's motto is a clear call to anglers: "Get hooked on us!"

Herb Garden Grilled Trout

Butter 3 tablespoons
White wine 1/4 cup, dry
Trout 4, cleaned
Salt and pepper to taste

Fresh herbs 1/3 cup, chopped, any combination of basil, thyme, dill and tarragon
Green onions 5, finely chopped

Melt butter and stir in wine. Generously brush each trout, inside and out. Sprinkle on salt and pepper. Spoon herbs and onions into fish cavities. Grill over charcoal, basting frequently. Cook until skin starts to crack and meat is white. Garnish with parsley and lemon.

Presidential Tabernash Trout

President Eisenhower reportedly had a fondness for fishing the Fraser River one mile downstream from Tabernash, an area designated Wild Trout water. Fresh trout baked with shrimp stuffing make this recipe well suited for a president, or anyone with a VIP appetite.

Trout fillets 4 pounds
Shrimp 20 large, steamed, peeled and chopped
Butter 1/2 cup, melted
Bread crumbs 1 1/2 cups, fresh
Fresh spinach 2 cups, chopped
Fresh parsley 1/2 cup, chopped

Green onion 6, thinly sliced
Salt and pepper to taste
Currants 3/4 cup (optional)
Water chestnuts 1/2 cup, diced
White wine 2 cups
Cider vinegar 2 tablespoons
Sugar 2 tablespoons

Slice fillets lengthwise, rinse, dry and set aside. In a large bowl, mix shrimp, melted butter, bread crumbs, spinach, parsley, green onion, salt, pepper, currants and water chestnuts. Spread stuffing on fillets. Roll each lengthwise, secure with toothpicks and arrange them in a large skillet. Mix together wine, vinegar and sugar. Pour mixture over fish, cover and poach for about 15 minutes or until fish is tender. Garnish with lemon wedges. Serves 6-8.

After visiting the Rocky Mountain state for the first time in 1902, President Theodore Roosevelt reportedly commented: "The scenery bankrupts the imagination." Needless to say, it was the first of many visits the president would make to Colorado.

Flat Tops Trout
and Mushrooms

East of the town of Meeker in the Flat Tops Wilderness awaits some of the finest fishing in the state, accessible only by foot or horseback.

Trout 4, cleaned with heads and tails left on
Flour 1/4 cup
Salt and pepper to taste
Butter 1/2 cup

Olive oil 3 tablespoons
Mushrooms 2 cups, sliced
Lemon juice 2 teaspoons
Green onions 10, thinly sliced
Bread crumbs 1/2 cup

Roll trout in flour and sprinkle with salt and pepper. Melt 3 tablespoons butter with oil over high heat, add trout and cook 4 minutes on each side. Transfer trout to platter. Melt 4 tablespoons of butter with mushrooms, add lemon juice, and saute 2 minutes. Remove mushrooms and butter to baking dish. Melt 1 tablespoon butter in skillet. Add green onions and bread crumbs. Saute until bread crumbs are toasty brown. Arrange trout on mushrooms in baking dish. Spread on bread-crumb mixture. Bake at 425° until trout flakes easily with a fork. Serves 4.

Every Fourth of July in Meeker, locals dress in costume and reenact an 1879 scene in which the Ute Indians clashed with the first white settlers. The town was named after Nathan C. Meeker, who came to the area after accepting a post at the White River Indian Agency. He was killed during the Indian attack in 1879. In addition to the July 4th reenactment, Meeker hosts a rodeo, dances, concerts, footraces and fireworks.

In the fall months, Meeker is flooded with elk and deer hunters, who meet in town before heading off to the Flat Top Mountains. And when hunting season comes to a close, anglers begin gearing up for trips to Flat Tops Wilderness' high-country lakes and streams.

Telluride Trout

Below the town of Telluride in southwestern Colorado, the rapid San Miguel River is stocked with foot-long rainbow trout.

Trout 6 whole, filleted and halved
Lemon juice from 1 lemon
Salt and pepper to taste
Eggs 5, whites only
Mayonnaise 1 1/3 cups
Cheese 1 1/3 cups, jack and/or cheddar, grated

Green onion 1/2 cup, chopped
Garlic powder 1/4 teaspoon
Parsley 1/4 cup, minced
Dill 2 tablespoons
Cayenne pepper 1/2 teaspoon
Parsley sprigs to garnish

Place fillets in well-greased broiling pan and sprinkle with lemon juice, salt and pepper. Broil on each side until fish begins to flake. In bowl, beat egg whites (at room temperature) until stiff. Fold in mayonnaise and remaining ingredients. Spread generously on each fillet and broil again until lightly browned.

Fishermen at Cherry Creek Reservoir State Recreation Area in central Colorado have reeled in more record fish than any other single body of water in the state. It has been dubbed as "one of Colorado's premier spots for large walleye."

Cherry Creek Walleye Creole

Butter 1/2 cup
Onion 1/2 cup, chopped
Celery 1 1/4 cups, diced
Carrots 1/2 cup, diced
Green pepper 1/4 cup, chopped
Red pepper 1/4 cup, chopped

Flour 1/2 cup
Tomatoes 12, chopped
Water 2/3 cup
Garlic powder 1 teaspoon
Cayenne 1/2 teaspoon
Walleye 1 pound, cooked fillets

Melt butter and saute vegetables. Blend in flour, tomatoes, water and spices. Stir until sauce boils and thickens. Reduce to simmer, add fish chunks and simmer 3 minutes. Serve over rice.

Bacon Bass

Despite the negative press against bacon's cholesterol, no one can deny the flavor-impact it has on bass. Maybe try a bacon substitute.

Bacon 5 slices
Onion 1 large, sliced
Garlic 2 cloves, minced
Tomatoes 8 medium, chopped
Dill 1 teaspoon

Oregano 1/2 teaspoon
Sugar 1/3 teaspoon
Parsley 2 tablespoons, minced
Salt and pepper to taste
Bass 1 2-pound, cleaned

Fry bacon, drain and crumble. Saute onion and garlic in bacon drippings. Stir in tomatoes, herbs and sugar; simmer five minutes. Place bass inside aluminum foil. Spread bacon inside cavity and sprinkle with salt and pepper. Spoon half the tomato mixture inside fish and pour the remainder over the top. Enclose the fish in foil and place on a baking sheet. Bake at 425° for about 30 minutes or until fish flakes easily with a fork.

Walnut Cream Bass

Fresh bass smothered in a cream sauce and garnished with walnuts.

Bass fillets 3 pounds, skinned
Salt and pepper to taste
Onion 1 medium, chopped
Celery 4 ribs, sliced
Mushrooms 1 1/2 cups, sliced
Butter 1/2 cup
Flour 1/4 cup

Salt 1/3 teaspoon
Dill 1/4 teaspoon
Basil 1 teaspoon
Dry mustard 1/3 teaspoon
Sugar 1/4 teaspoon
Half and half 2 1/2 cups
Walnuts 3/4 cup, chopped

Sprinkle fillets with salt and pepper and place skin-side down on foil-lined pan. Saute onion, celery and mushrooms in butter until onion is translucent. Stir in flour, salt, dill, basil, mustard and sugar. Cook 2 minutes. Slowly stir in cream. Keep stirring till sauce thickens. Pour over fish. Bake at 325° for 35 minutes or until fish flakes easily with a fork. Sprinkle with walnuts and broil for about three minutes.

Kokanee with Cucumber Sauce

Colorado's largest natural body of water, Grand Lake is known for its rainbow trout, mackinaw and kokanee salmon.

Kokanee enough for 8 steaks
Salt 2 tablespoons
Lemon juice from 1 lemon
Cucumber 1 large
Sour cream 3/4 cup
Mayonnaise 1/3 cup

Onion 1/8 cup, grated
Parsley 2 tablespoons, minced
Garlic powder 1/2 teaspoon
Cider vinegar 1 tablespoon
Salt and pepper to taste
Lemon wedges for garnish

Half fill a large skillet with water. Add two tablespoons salt, juice of one lemon and bring to a boil. Simmer fish steaks 10 minutes, remove with a slotted spoon and refrigerate. Grate cucumber into a bowl and add remaining ingredients (except lemon wedges); chill thoroughly. Spoon sauce over steaks and garnish with lemon.

Time is but the stream I go a-fishing in.

—Henry David Thoreau

Fish a la Fryingpan

In Aspen, not only are fish cooked in a frying pan, they are hooked in the Fryingpan River. Silly name, maybe--but the river earns a "Gold Medal" designation for its abundance of rainbow and brown trout.

Trout 2 pounds, filleted
Eggs 2, beaten
Milk 3 tablespoons
Salt and pepper to taste
Garlic powder 1/4 teaspoon

Onion Powder 1/4 teaspoon
Dill 1/4 teaspoon
Cracker crumbs 1/2 cup
Peanut oil 1 cup
Lemon wedges for garnish

Slice fish into strips. In a bowl, whisk eggs, milk, herbs and spices. Dip fish into egg, then cracker crumbs, back into egg, then crumbs, until well coated. Fry in hot peanut oil until golden. Drain on paper towel. Serve with lemon wedges and tartar sauce.

Red Lion Inn Spaetzle

A mountain setting provides the backdrop for the Red Lion Inn, minutes from Boulder in north central Colorado. The wooden, turn-of-the-century lodge is recommended for its charm and menu offering elegant wild game entrees.

Flour 1 pound
Eggs 6
Salt 1 tablespoon

Nutmeg 1/4 teaspoon
Water 2 cups

In a mixing bowl, combine flour and eggs. Add salt and nutmeg. Mix in water slowly, until it achieves consistency of heavy pancake batter. Using a spaetzle machine or kitchen colander, drip batter into boiling water. Allow noodles to cook until floating--about 5 minutes. Remove from water and put in ice water to cool. Drain well. Just before serving, saute spaetzle in butter. Serves 8.

For those with a taste for German beer, brats, music, polkas and yodeling at high altitudes, September is the time to head to Vail, Montrose, Glenwood Springs, Snowmass, and a host of other Colorado towns celebrating "Oktoberfests."

Gourmet Goulash Casserole

Diane M. Boone—Loveland, Colorado

Hamburger 1 1/2 pounds
Onion 1/2 medium, chopped
Salt to taste
Pepper to taste
Minced garlic to taste

Tomatoes 1 (28 oz.) can, whole, peeled
Cream of mushroom soup 1 can
Wide egg noodles 8 ounces, cooked, drained and rinsed

Brown meat and onion. Drain off grease. Add seasonings. Add tomatoes with liquid. Simmer 45 minutes. Remove from heat. When mixture stops boiling, blend in soup. Mix in cooked, drained and rinsed egg noodles. Pour into casserole. If desired, add shredded cheese, mixing 1/2 cup into the casserole and sprinkling 3/4 cup on top. Cover and bake at 350° for 30 minutes. Serves 4-6.

Zucchini Lasagne

Ethel Montgomery—Lamar, Colorado: "I like using zucchini because it's more healthful and less expensive to buy than meat, and so easily grown in the garden."

Zucchini 4 medium
Ground beef or venison
  1 pound (1 cup of ham
  or chicken may be substituted)
Garlic 2 cloves, minced
Thyme 1/2 teaspoon
Oregano 1/2 teaspoon
Seasoning salt 1/2 teaspoon
Butter 2 tablespoons

Flour 2 tablespoons
Tomato juice 1 1/2 cups
Salt and pepper to taste
Mozzarella cheese 1 cup,
  shredded
Cheddar cheese 1/2 cup,
  shredded
Potato chips 1/2 cup, crushed

Cut zucchini lengthwise into 1/4-inch slices. Fry meat and drain off grease. Saute garlic, thyme, oregano and seasoning salt in the butter for about two minutes, stirring continuously as it will scorch easily. Blend in flour. Add tomato juice and cook to thicken. Salt and pepper to taste. Into a greased 9x13 pan, layer zucchini, meat and cheese. Repeat layers, reserving 1/2 cup cheese. Pour sauce over all. Cover with foil and bake at 350° for 45 minutes. Remove foil, top with potato chips and cheese. Bake an additional 10 minutes.

A saying shared amongst ski racers: "Eat pasta... go 'fasta'."

Pasta Pesto

Fresh basil 3 cups, packed
Fresh parsley 3/4 cup, packed
Garlic 3 cloves
Parmesan 1 cup, grated
Pine nuts or walnuts 2/3 cup

Olive oil 2/3 cup
Butter 2 tablespoons, melted
Salt to taste
Pepper freshly ground
Pasta 1 pound, cooked, drained

Puree all pesto ingredients in blender until smooth. Pour over pasta and toss lightly to coat evenly. Garnish with a sprinkle of parmesan and dash of pepper. Serves 4.

Mexican Favorites

Following the Mexican War and the Treaty of Guadalupe Hidalgo in 1848, the victorious U.S. treaty signers agreed to honor Mexican land grants in southern Colorado. The first Hispanic settlers arrived in 1852, establishing the first permanent town in the state--San Luis. The Mexican culture retains a strong presence in this area and has spread to other pockets throughout the state. Probably the most obvious contribution, aside from Spanish-Mexican place names that dominate the state, is the ever-present influence of south-of-the-border cuisine, which has been a favorite of Coloradans long before Mexican restaurants began popping up in cities and suburbs nationwide.

Coloradans are uninhibited in their use of chile peppers and cayenne; tortillas replace bread on the dining table--used to soak up sauces and forever being wrapped around any combination of beans, meat, vegetables and cheese. For the newcomer's tender tastebuds, some dishes may leave a bit of a burn, but take heart: Chile-pepper tolerance is proportionate to consumption.

Green Chile Enchiladas

Meatless and full of cheese, these are a year-round favorite.

Butter 1/3 cup
Flour 1/3 cup
Half-and-half 2 1/2 cups
Green chiles 1 (7 oz.) can
Onion 1/2 cup, minced
Cayenne 1/8 teaspoon

Cheddar cheese 4 cups, grated
Jack cheese 4 cups, grated
Onion 1 medium, minced
Oil for frying
Corn tortillas 12
Sour cream 2 cups

Melt butter in small saucepan and sprinkle in flour. When flour is slightly browned and begins to bubble, slowly stir in half-and-half. Simmer, stirring regularly for 5 minutes. Add chiles, onion and cayenne, and simmer 10 minutes. Mix cheeses with onion. Dip each tortilla into hot oil for 5 seconds and drain on paper towel. Scoop cheese mixture onto each tortilla, roll up and place in baking pan. Top with green chile sauce, sprinkle on remaining cheese and broil until bubbly. Garnish generously with sour cream. Serves 6.

Enchilada Casserole

Sharon Galligar Chance—Colorado Springs, Colorado: "This dish gains flavor if prepared in advance and reheated. Freezes well, too."

Ground meat 2 pounds
Onion 1 small
Salsa 1 small jar, medium hot
Cream of mushroom soup 2 cans
Tomatoes 1 can, diced

Corn tortillas 1 package
Cheddar cheese 1 pound, grated
Black olives 1 (4 oz.) can, sliced
Green onions 3, chopped

Brown meat and onion together. Drain excess liquid and add salsa. Simmer together for 10 minutes. In a saucepan, blend soup and tomatoes, and bring to a boil. Line the bottom of a greased, 9x13 casserole dish with a layer of tortillas. Spread half the meat over tortillas and sprinkle on one-third the cheese, and cover with half the soup mixture. Add another layer of tortillas, meat, cheese and soup. Top with a final layer of cheese, sprinkled with sliced olives and green onions. Cover pan with foil and bake at 350° for 15 minutes. Uncover and bake 15 minutes longer. Serves 6-8.

Tacoritas

This recipe is shared by Junelle Pringle, owner of Waunita Hot Springs Ranch, in Gunnison, Colorado.

Cream of chicken soup 3 cans
Water 2 soup cans
Chili powder 2 tablespoons
Onion powder 1 tablespoon
Sage one teaspoon (optional)

Cumin 1 teaspoon
Ground beef 2 pounds, lean
Onion 1 medium, chopped
Flour tortillas package of 8-inch
Cheese 1 cup, grated

Make sauce by blending first 6 ingredients. Brown meat in onions. Add one-quarter of the sauce to meat. Spoon 1/2 cup of meat mixture into each tortilla. Fold each tortilla like an envelope and place, fold-side down, in greased baking pan. Pour remaining sauce over tortillas. Top with cheese and bake at 350° for 30 minutes, until cheese is golden and bubbly. Serves 10.

Turkey Enchiladas

A Mexican favorite prepared by Judy Clemmer at the Leadville Country Inn, a historic 1893 Queen Anne style bed-and-breakfast offering romantic moonlit sleighrides and elegant candlelight dinners.

Onion 1 1/4 cup, chopped
Garlic salt 1 teaspoon
Vegetable oil 2 tablespoons
Flour 1 tablespoon
Tomatoes 1 (16 oz.) can
Tomato sauce 1 (15 oz.) can
Green chiles 1 (4 oz.) can
Sugar 1 teaspoon

Cumin 1 teaspoon
Salt 1/4 teaspoon
Turkey 2 cups, cooked
and shredded
Cheddar cheese 1 1/2 cups,
grated
Olives 1/4 cup, chopped
Flour tortillas

Cook 3/4 cup onions and garlic salt in oil until tender, but not brown. Stir in flour, tomatoes, tomato sauce, green chiles, sugar, cumin and salt. Cook until thick and bubbly. Mix turkey, cheese, olives, 1/4 cup onions and half the sauce mixture. Spoon this mixture into flour tortillas, roll into enchiladas and place in baking dish. Pour remaining sauce over top, sprinkle with remaining cheese and onion. Bake at 350° until cheese is bubbly.

Tamale Pie

Ground beef 1 pound
Onion 1 medium, chopped
Garlic salt 1 teaspoon
Chili powder 1 teaspoon
Cayenne dash
Salt and pepper to taste
Tomato sauce 2 cups

Tomatoes 1 (16 oz.) can
Black olives 1 (7 oz.) can,
sliced
Rice 1 cup, cooked
Corn 1 16-ounce can
Corn meal 3/4 cup
Jack cheese 1 cup, grated

Brown hamburger with onion and spices. Drain and add remaining ingredients, except cheese. Mix well and bake at 350° for 45 minutes to one hour. Sprinkle cheese over the top and bake until melted and bubbly. Serves 4-6.

Rosita Rellenos

In 1873, rich silver deposits were discovered in Rosita, sending miners for the first time to the Wet Mountain Valley in south central Colorado.

Stewed tomatoes 1 (16 oz.) can
Green chiles 2 (4 oz.) cans, whole, mild
Jack cheese 3/4 pound
Eggs 3, separated
Baking powder 3/4 teaspoon

Flour 1 tablespoon
Onion powder 1/2 teaspoon
Cayenne dash
Vegetable oil for frying
Cheddar cheese 1/4 pound, shredded

Simmer tomatoes for about 50 minutes to reduce juice. Blot chiles with paper towel. Cut cheese into rectangles and insert one in each chile. Beat egg whites with baking powder and in separate bowl beat yolks with flour, onion powder and cayenne. Gently fold whites into yolks. Dip chiles into egg, then into hot oil. Turn once until golden all around. Arrange chiles on baking dish. Pour tomatoes over all. Bake at 300° for 20 minutes. Sprinkle grated cheese over top and bake 5-10 minutes longer, until bubbly.

Cortez Chimis

Lying in the Montezuma Valley, where the high desert and the San Juan Mountains meet, is the city of Cortez, a popular tourist stop in the southwest region of Colorado.

Chicken breasts 2 whole
Onion 1 large, chopped
Butter 2 tablespoons
Cheese 3/4 cup, shredded
Salsa 1/2 cup
Cilantro 1/4 cup, chopped

Green chiles 1/4 cup, diced
Margarine 3/4 cup melted
Tortillas 1 dozen, flour
Lettuce 1/2 head, shredded
Sour cream to garnish
Tomatoes 2 large, chopped

Skin, cook and shred chicken. Saute onions in butter, mix with chicken and add cheese, salsa, cilantro and chiles. Brush margarine on both sides of each tortilla. Spoon filling down center of each tortilla, roll up and place seam side down on foil-lined baking sheet. Bake at 500° for 10 minutes until golden brown. Serve chimis on shredded lettuce. Top with sour cream and tomatoes. Serves 8-12.

Dianne's Black Bean and Buffalo Chili

Dianne Eschman—Telluride, Colorado: "Serve with fresh cilantro and sour cream. Good with hot, baked corn bread."

Peanut oil 2 tablespoons
Onions 2 large
Garlic 2 cloves, minced
Buffalo roast 2 1/2 pounds, into small pieces
Masa harina 1/4 cup
Plum tomatoes 1 can, chopped with juice
Stock 4 cups, chicken or beef
Chile powder 6 tablespoons

Cumin 1 tablespoon
Oregano 1 teaspoon
Cinnamon 1 teaspoon
Pepper 1 teaspoon, fresh, ground
Salt 1 teaspoon or to taste
Cider vinegar 2 tablespoons
Jalapeno peppers 2 fresh, seeded, deveined and chopped
Black beans 4 cups, cooked
Cilantro 1 bunch, chopped

In a large saute pan or Dutch oven, heat oil over moderate heat until rippling. Add onions and saute, stirring frequently until golden brown. Add garlic. Saute, stirring frequently, for 2 minutes more. Add buffalo and cook until meat loses red color, stirring frequently. Sprinkle on masa harina, stirring well, until cooked through, about 2 minutes. Stir in remaining ingredients, except black beans. Turn heat to high simmer. Add beans. Reduce heat. Cook about 1 hour and add chopped cilantro. Continue cooking for 1-2 hours longer, until flavors are well blended.

Named after a Russian princess, the San Sophia bed-and-breakfast caters to guests in need of a luxurious retreat. The inn is less than a block from the ski slopes of Telluride and within walking distance of hiking in the majestic mountains surrounding the town. Each room in the San Sophia is named after one of the area's mines, and features brass beds, antique decor and luxurious baths. Breakfasts are served indoors or out, but always in the midst of Telluride's phenomenal scenery.

Dacra Dollies Chili

Mary Weiler—Durango, Colorado: "This recipe was handed down to me from my mother, an Irish woman with a Mexican flair. The recipe won us first place in the First Annual Four Corners Chili Cook-Off held in Durango in May."

Bacon 5 slices
Italian sausage 1/2 pound, ground
Top sirloin 1 1/2 pounds, cubed
Onion 1, chopped
Green pepper 1 small, chopped
Garlic 1 clove, minced

Jalapenos 2 chopped
Chili powder 1 1/2 tablespoons
Crushed red pepper 1/2 teaspoon
Salt 1/2 teaspoon
Oregano 1/4 teaspoon
Water 2 1/2 cups
Tomato paste 1 (12 oz.) can

Cook bacon till crisp; drain and crumble. Discard drippings and set bacon aside. Brown sausage in same pan. Drain off grease, reserving 2 tablespoons. Set sausage aside. Brown sirloin, onions, green pepper and garlic in reserved drippings. Add cooked bacon, sausage, jalapenos, chili powder, crushed red pepper, salt and oregano. Stir in water and tomato paste. Bring to a boil; simmer uncovered for 1 1/2 hours, stirring occasionally. Serves 6-8.

NOTE: Dacra is an acronym for Durango Area Chamber Resort Association.

Colorado winters may be chilly, but come spring and summer its "chili" of another sort... Grand Junction heats things up in May with the Western Colorado District Chili Cookoff with chili chefs competing for prizes. Likewise, Steamboat Springs greets June with the annual Ambassador's Chili Cookoff and Pepper Roast, highlighting Ms. Hot 'n Spicy and Hoot 'n Holler competitions. By July, the heat is on in Snowmass, where restaurants prepare their fiery entrees during the annual Chili Shoot-Out. For those with a chili passion, the ultimate Chili Cookoff brings more than 100 regional cooks to Colorado Springs each June to compete for the state title.

Mexirado Pizza

World's apart, Mexican and Italian cooking meet in Colorado with this tortilla-pizza recipe. Serve them as a meal with a salad, or sliced for appetizers. Always good with sour cream, guacamole and salsa.

Tortillas 1 dozen, flour
Spaghetti sauce or Salsa 2 cups
Chicken 5 breasts, grilled and
  sliced in strips
Onion 1 medium, thinly sliced
Green chiles 1 (4 oz.) can, diced

Cilantro 1/4 cup, minced
Oil 3 tablespoons
Cheese 1 1/2 cups, jack and
  cheddar, shredded
Tomatoes 3 medium, chopped

Spread tortillas on ungreased cookie sheets and bake at 400° for five minutes, until toasted. Turn tortillas over, spread about two tablespoons of sauce on each, add desired amounts of chicken strips, onion, green chiles and cilantro. Lightly sprinkle with oil, top with shredded cheese. Bake until cheese starts to bubble, about 15 minutes. Note: Vegetarians can substitute beans and minced vegetables for the chicken.

Ouray Enchiladas

Stuffed with Swiss cheese, these enchiladas are named after the tiny mining mountain town of Ouray, sometimes referred to as the "Switzerland of the United States" because of its dramatic alpine setting.

Chili powder 6 tablespoons
Stock 2 cups, chicken or beef
Vegetable oil 4 tablespoons
Flour 4 tablespoons
Cilantro 3 tablespoons, chopped
Salt to taste

Vegetable oil 1/4 cup
Tortillas 8, corn
Swiss cheese 2 cups, shredded
Black olives 2/3 cup, diced
Sour cream 3/4 cup
Green onions 5, chopped

Dissolve chili powder in stock. Heat 4 tablespoons oil in saucepan, add flour and brown slightly. Slowly stir in stock and spices. Simmer till thick. Heat oil and dip tortillas in just to soften. Sprinkle cheese, olives and sauce into middle of tortillas. Roll up and cover with sauce. Garnish with sour cream and onions.

Boulder Burritos

An hour north of Denver, at the base of the dramatic rock formations known as the Flatirons, is Boulder, a utopia for outdoor enthusiasts. Life here evolves around mountain biking, hiking, rock climbing... the list is endless. For the healthy appetite with little time to worry about balancing a meal, these burritos are filling, easy to prepare, and provide nutrition from every food group. Leftovers are easily wrapped, packed and especially satisfying on the trail.

Chicken 1 fryer, cut in parts
Olive oil 3 tablespoons
Garlic 3 cloves, minced
Onion 1 medium, chopped
Carrot 1 large, finely chopped
Tomatoes 3 fresh, chopped
Cumin 1/4 teaspoon
Chili powder 2 tablespoons
Cayenne to taste

Salt and pepper to taste
Cilantro 1/2 cup, chopped
Green chiles 1 (4 oz.) can, diced
Jalapenos 1/3 cup, diced
Flour tortillas 8-12
Cheese 1 1/2 cups, cheddar
 and jack, shredded
Lettuce 2 cups, shredded
Sour cream to garnish

Boil chicken, cook and shred to make about 3 cups. Set aside. In large pan, heat oil and saute garlic, onion and carrot for about 5 minutes. Stir in tomatoes. With back side of spoon, crush tomatoes to release juices. Add cumin, chili powder, cayenne, salt, pepper and 1/4 cup cilantro. Simmer 10 minutes. Stir in green chiles, jalapenos and chicken, and simmer 15 minutes longer. As this cooks, lightly sprinkle water on tortillas and wrap them in foil or cotton towel. Heat tortillas at 200°. Spoon chicken mixture into center of tortilla, add cheese, cilantro, sour cream and lettuce. Fold up one end and roll. Garnish with shredded lettuce, sour cream, salsa and guacamole.

Margarita Fajitas

A favorite Coloradan pastime: gathering with friends for a cookout. This recipe adds a dash of lime juice and tequila to give fajitas an extra zing. With a buffet of fresh, shredded veggies, they are a meal unto themselves. Teamed with freshly blended margaritas and a good circle of friends, this cookout can turn into a midsummer celebration.

Beef or chicken 3 pounds
Oil 2 tablespoons
Chili powder 1 tablespoon
Jalapenos 1/4 cup, diced
Garlic powder 2 teaspoons
Onion powder 2 teaspoons
Cayenne to taste
Salt and pepper to taste
Salsa 1/2 cup
Tequila 1/4 cup
Lime juice from 1 lime

Sugar 1 tablespoon
Onions 2 large, thinly slices
Green peppers 2 large, sliced
Mushrooms 1 pound, sliced
Oil 1/4 cup
Flour tortillas 2 dozen
Lettuce 1 large head, shredded
Garnish: Olives, sour cream
  shredded cheese, salsa, guaca-
  mole, chopped tomatoes, refried
  beans, diced green chiles

Arrange meat in a baking dish. Combine together: 1 tablespoon oil, chili powder, jalapenos, garlic and onion powders, cayenne, salt, pepper, salsa, tequila, lime and sugar. Pour marinade over meat and refrigerate several hours or overnight. When ready to prepare, grill meat, occasionally basting with marinade. As meat is grilling, saute onions, peppers and mushrooms in oil. Season to taste. Set table with grilled, sliced meat, bowl of sauteed vegetables, and platter of garnishes. Each person can create their own fajitas by spooning meat mixture into center of tortilla, adding garnishes and folding or rolling.

Waunita Tostadas

Junelle Pringle—Waunita Ranch Hot Springs, Gunnison, Colorado

Ground beef 1 pound, lean
Onion 1 cup, chopped
Chili powder 1 1/2 teaspoons
Salt 1 teaspoon
Tomatoes 2 large, chopped
Tomatillos 1 (7 oz.) can
Green chiles 1 (4 oz.) can, diced

Pinto beans 1 (16 oz.) can
Corn 1 can, whole-kernel
Oregano 1 tablespoon
Salad oil enough for frying
Corn tortillas 8
Lettuce 1 head, shredded
Cheese 2 cups, jack, shredded

In large skillet, combine ground beef, onions, chili powder and salt. Cook over medium-high heat until beef is browned (about 10 minutes), stirring occasionally. Drain off grease. Stir in tomatoes and drained tomatillos and green chiles. Reduce heat to medium and cook 15 minutes, stirring occasionally. Stir in drained pinto beans and corn. Add oregano and cook 5 minutes longer. In small skillet, heat one inch of oil over high heat. Place tortilla in the oil, about 30 seconds on each side. Drain on paper towel. Repeat with remaining tortillas. To serve: layer one cup shredded lettuce, 3/4 cup beef mixture and 1/4 cup shredded cheese onto each tortilla.

Taco Casserole

Junelle Pringle—Waunita Ranch Hot Springs, Gunnison, Colorado

Ground beef 2 pounds, lean
Onion 1 large, chopped
Evaporated milk 1 can
Cream of chicken soup 1 can
Cream of mushroom soup 1 can

Enchilada sauce 1 cup
Pinto beans 16-ounce can
Green chiles 1 (4 oz.) can, chopped
Tortilla chips 11-ounce bag
Cheese 4 cups, grated

Brown beef and onion in skillet. In saucepan, heat milk, soups, enchilada sauce and green chiles until bubbly. Crush the tortilla chips and spread half into a lightly greased 9x13 casserole dish. Cover with half of the meat, sauce and cheese. Repeat the layers. Bake at 350° for 30 minutes, or until bubbly.

Alamosa Taco Sauce

Vicki Copper—Alamosa, Colorado: "This is very good with any Mexican dish and makes a delicious dip with nacho chips."

Onions 3 peeled and chopped
Tomatoes 5 quarts, peeled and chopped in blender
Green chiles 1 cup, chopped
Cumin 1 tablespoon

Garlic powder 1/2 teaspoon
White vinegar 1 1/2 cups
Sugar 1/2 cup
Red pepper 3/4 to 1 teaspoon
Salt 2 tablespoons

Bring all ingredients to a rolling boil. Simmer for one hour and pack into pint jars. Process in boiling water bath for 20 minutes. If you wish to use quart jars, process for 30 minutes. May be served immediately and will keep up to two years in sealed jars.

PEPPERS

Past and Present

Historians of the culinary arts believe that hundreds of years ago the Pueblo Indians began tossing fiery chile peppers into their stews to add flavor. Today, dozens of varieties of peppers exist, ranging in size and color, flavor and hotness. One simple rule of thumb for gauging spice amplitude: The smaller the pepper, the holler. Other ways to prevent searing the tongue are to cut out the seeds and whitish interiors before chopping a pepper--the seeds and internal skin carry superior quantities of tongue-burning oils. What to do in case of a mouth-overdose? We've yet to find a remedy backed by medical or science experts, or even one method agreed upon by pepper aficionados. Some swear alcohol consumption is the cure, others drink jugs of water and suck ice cubes. To each his own. Finally, one more word to the wise: To avoid a tear-jerker meal... never touch eyes with fingers that have been handling chile peppers.

On The Side

It seems belittling to label these recipes as "side dishes." Many are so hearty they could stand up to any meal, let alone serve as a main course. Nevertheless, we offer a wide selection, beginning with beans--a staple food for Colorado's Anasazi Indians, cowboys, miners, and the 20th-century gourmet cook.

Cripple Creek Beans 'n' Gold

Jean I. Stillwell—Colorado Springs, Colorado: "This is a great side dish with barbecues, picnics or a main meal. Oranges are the Cripple Creek "gold" ingredient. Leftovers can be stored, reheated and revived with a bit of salsa or tomato sauce."

Campbell's Pork 'n' Beans® 1 (28 oz.) can
Oranges 3, sliced; remove zest from 1 and save

Brown sugar or molasses 1/4 cup
Bacon or ham 1/2 pound, sliced
Mustard several tablespoons
Salsa 1/4 to 1/2 cup

Mix beans, orange zest, half the brown sugar or molasses, and salsa. Put the remaining sugar or molasses on one side of each slice of orange. Spread mustard on one side of each slice of bacon or ham. Line a baking dish with the bacon (or ham) and cover with several slices of orange. Add the bean mixture and use remaining bacon (or ham) on top of beans, alternating with the orange and the meat and beginning on the outer edge of the pan. Bake at 350° for 30 to 45 minutes. Add salt and pepper to taste. Serves 5.

In 1893, a silver crash devastated Colorado's economy. That is, until gold was discovered at Cripple Creek--known as Colorado's last and greatest mining camp. The rush to Cripple Creek saved the state from absolute depression and helped create another two dozen millionaires.

Cowboy Baked Beans

At the Prospector Restaurant in Leadville, beans are served from a large black kettle kept warm over an open flame next to the fireplace. This recipe is one of the most requested.

Pork and beans 2 (18 oz.) cans
Ketchup 1 cup
Brown sugar 1/4 to 1/2 cup
Worcestershire 2 tablespoons
Mustard 1 tablespoon

Onion 1/2 cup, finely chopped
Jalapeno pepper 1 teaspoon, pickled, finely chopped
Bacon 2 strips, raw

Mix all ingredients together except for bacon. Pour into a two-quart casserole. Top with bacon. Bake at 350° for approximately one hour. Remove bacon and stir before serving. Serves 6-8.

Ham Hocks and Black-eyed Peas

Carneice Brown-White—Denver, Colorado: "This is a traditional family New Year's dish. The peas denote good luck. We serve it at dinner with pork, sweet potatoes and greens."

Black-eyed peas 2 cups, dried
Ham hocks 4, smoked
Onion 1 medium, chopped
Crushed red pepper 1 tablespoon
Salt and pepper to taste

Bay leaves 2
Celery 1 stalk
Garlic salt 1 teaspoon
Sugar 1/2 teaspoon
Dry mustard 1 teaspoon.
Okra 1 package, frozen

Soak peas overnight. Place ham hocks in a pot and add enough water to cover. Bring to a boil and reduce heat. Simmer until done. In colander, wash black-eyed peas under cold running water. In a large pot, combine the peas with all other ingredients, except okra. Simmer until peas are tender and the liquid is almost absorbed. Place okra on top of peas, but do not stir. Cover and cook for 15 minutes, until okra is tender. Serves 6-8.

Green Cheese Rice

Not to worry--there really isn't green cheese in this recipe. It's just the combination of green pepper and cheese.

Rice 2 cups
Garlic 2 cloves, minced
Onions 1 large, finely chopped
Parsley 1 cup fresh, chopped
Cheese 2 cups, shredded
Green peppers 2, chopped

Evaporated milk 2 cups
Oil 2/3 cup
Eggs 2, beaten
Cayenne a dash
Salt and pepper to taste

Cook the rice. Mix together the remaining ingredients and pour into a lightly greased baking dish. Bake in 350° oven for 20 minutes.

To eat is human, to digest divine.

— Charles T. Copeland

Almond Fried Rice

An extended-family favorite, courtesy of Waunita Hot Springs Ranch.

Rice 8 cups
Salt 1 tablespoon
Salad oil 1/2 cup
Pepper 1/2 tablespoon
Garlic 2 cloves

Green pepper 2 cups, chopped
Onion 2 cups, chopped
Soy sauce 1/2 cup
Almonds 1 1/2 cups,
  chopped or slivered

Cook the rice accordingly and set aside. In a skillet, sprinkle salt over salad oil and add remaining ingredients except soy sauce and almonds. Saute until onions are translucent. Transfer rice to a casserole dish. Pour sauce over top. Add soy sauce and almonds. Toss to mix. Bake in 350° oven for 30 minutes, tossing often.

Wild Rice Casserole

Marjorie Gleason—Pueblo, Colorado

Veal or pork steak 1 1/2 pounds, cubed
Onion 1 small, chopped
Chicken and rice soup 1 can
Cream of mushroom soup 1 can
Water 1 soup can

Mushrooms 1 can
White rice 1/2 cup, uncooked
Wild rice 1/4 cup, soaked overnight in water
Celery 1 cup, chopped
Soy sauce 1 tablespoon

Brown meat and onions. Add remaining ingredients and mix together well. Place in a two-quart casserole dish. Bake at 350° for 1 1/2 hours. Serves 12.

Can you inform me of any other pleasure which can be enjoyed three times a day, and equally in old age as in youth?

—Charles Maurice Talleyrand Perigord

Rice Radroni

June Santore—Radroni, Colorado

Butter 1/3 cup
Onion 1/4 cup, chopped
Celery 1 2/3 cup, chopped
Corn 3 3/4 cups, fresh or frozen
Cheddar cheese 3 cups, grated

Milk 1 1/2 cups
Rice 1 1/4 cups, cooked
Salt and pepper to taste
Cayenne a dash

Melt butter in skillet. Add onion and celery and saute about 5 minutes. Add remaining ingredients, stirring well after each new addition. Remove from heat. Butter a two-quart casserole dish. Pour in rice mixture. Cover and bake at 325° for about 50 minutes.

Posole de Pueblo

Amelia V. Smith—Pueblo, Colorado: "Stew may be eaten with warm flour tortillas on a cold, wintry day. Keeps well in the freezer."

Pork hocks 2 pounds
Pork shoulder 3 pounds, cut in
   2-inch chunks
Salt 2-3 tablespoons, to taste
Garlic 2 large cloves, minced
Hominy 2 pounds, frozen prepared,
   exclusively for posole

Powdered red chile
   6 tablespoons, mild or hot
Oregano 3 teaspoons,
   whole-leaf (optional)

Place meat and pork hocks in a large Dutch oven. Add five quarts water, or enough to cover the meat. Add one tablespoon salt and one minced garlic clove. Bring to a boil. Cook slowly till meat is tender, about 1 1/2 hours. Rinse the hominy and add to meat. Again add water to cover meat and hominy. Boil over low-medium heat for 30 minutes. Add remaining salt, garlic, chile and oregano. Simmer for about two hours, or until hominy pops open like popcorn and meat is tender. Discard the bones before serving. Serves 12-14.

Charlene's Chinese Rice

Charlene Sikorsy—Aurora, Colorado: "As good as the restaurants!"

Peanut oil 3 tablespoon
Eggs 2
Onion 1 small, chopped
Green onions 3, thinly sliced
Carrots 1/4 cup, minced
Bean sprouts 1 cup, fresh

Chicken stock base
   2 tablespoons
Soy sauce 1/4 cup
Cayenne a dash (optional)
Rice 3 1/2 cups, cooked
Salt and pepper to taste

In a large skillet or wok, heat oil over high heat. Add unbeaten eggs and scramble quickly into small chunks. Add onion, green onions and carrots, and stir fry for two minutes. Add remaining ingredients and stir fry until heated throughout. Serves 6.

Loveland Corn Cakes

A main dish for brunch or excellent side dish at dinner.

Cornmeal 1/4 cups
Flour 1 1/4 cups
Salt 1/2 teaspoon
Baking powder 2 1/4 teaspoons
Eggs 1 whole, 1 white
Milk 1 cups

Butter 2 tablespoons
Corn 1 cup, cut fresh off the cob
Salt and pepper to taste
Dill 1 teaspoon, fresh, minced
Butter as desired
Sour cream 2/3 cup

Sift together cornmeal, flour, salt and baking powder. Add eggs and milk. Blend thoroughly. Melt butter and add to batter. Stir in fresh corn and dill. Add salt and pepper to taste. Pour batter into greased, hot skillet. When top of cakes bubble, turn and cook the other side. Serve cakes warm, with butter and sour cream.

Each Valentine's Day, American sweet-hearts send their letters to loved ones with the town of Loveland's postmark. But long before cards began circulating through town, the area was known for its cherry orchards and the corn, which some say grew to "ten-feet high." Every bit as popular with the white settlers as the Native Americans before them, the golden crop was paid tribute to by the locals with a free-feed Corn Roast Day, inaugurated in 1894.

Corn in Sour Cream Sauce

A flavorful, elegant and simple side dish.

Butter 1/4 cup
Corn 6 ears, boiled
Green pepper 3 tablespoons, minced
Red pepper 3 tablespoons, minced
Onion 1/4 cup, chopped

Flour 1 tablespoon
Cayenne a dash (optional)
Garlic powder 1/4 teaspoon
Salt and pepper to taste
Sour cream 1 cup, well chilled
Paprika to garnish

Melt half the butter in skillet. Slice fresh corn off the ears and add it to the butter, frying until crispy and slightly browned. Remove from heat. Add peppers and onions. Cook slowly, stirring frequently. Sprinkle in flour and spices and stir well. Add sour cream by heaping spoonfuls, blending well after each addition. Continue to simmer until it thickens. Spoon sauce over corn and garnish with paprika.

Corn, or "maize" in the native language, was the most important crop of Indians throughout North and South America. In the West, Indians performed ceremonial corn dances during the growing season in order to inspire the good spirits to bless them with a bountiful harvest. The dance was also believed to ward off evil spirits. To the Indian way of thinking, corn was also thought of as having miraculous powers and many folk stories were told of its origins. One such example: Some tribes tell a tale of a large turkey hen flying over their territory and dropping ears of blue corn from its wings. The corn took to seed, the seed to sprouts, and eventually the Indians took to the field to harvest their first crop of maize.

Corn-stuffed Tomatoes

The flavor of fresh, homegrown vegetables is unbeatable.

Tomatoes 6, ripe, firm
Salt
Butter 6 tablespoons
Onion 1/4 cup, chopped
Green pepper 3 tablespoons,
  finely chopped
Cayenne a dash

Parmesan cheese 1 cup, grated
Corn cut fresh off the cob to
  make about 4 cups
Dill 1 teaspoon, dry, or
  1 tablespoon, fresh, minced
Salt and pepper to taste
Sour cream to garnish

Core tomatoes, scrape out insides and salt well. Melt butter. Saute onion and pepper in butter. Stir in remaining ingredients, except the sour cream. Heat through. Remove from heat and cool five minutes. Stuff each tomato with corn mixture. Place tomatoes in a baking dish with just enough water in it to cover bottom. Bake at 375° for about 20-25 minutes, until tops of tomatoes start to brown.

Remember the Tomalamo!

"Drink beer; hit a Texan!" That's the battle cry of Coloradans gearing up for the annual Tomalamo in Twin Lakes. For one weekend each September, Coloradans and Texans go to combat, carrying cases and cases of rotten tomatoes... the hand grenades and only ammunition used in the treacherous Tomato War. The rules of the war are such: Once a soldier has been pelted by a tomato, they must exit the battle scene and rely on the allies to win the war. But... what's the point? To drink beer, run in the mountains, have fun, and cream the competition with nasty, rotten tomatoes.

Zucchini Bake

This recipe is the creation of two gourmet gals—Marian Hilzer of Greeley, Colorado, and Nan Forbush of San Diego, California.

Zucchini 1 large, about 10 inches long
Ground beef 1 pound
Salt 1/4 teaspoon
Pepper 1/4 teaspoon
Egg 1
Soda crackers 10 small
Cheese 1/4 pound, shredded

Cut zucchini lengthwise. Remove seeds and set them aside. Mix together ground beef, salt, pepper, egg and crackers. Stir in the seeds. Spoon mixture into the zucchini shell. Bake at 400° for one hour. Just before serving, sprinkle cheese on top and bake an additional 10 to 15 minutes. The stuffed zucchini can be stored in the freezer to be served at a later date. Serves 6.

Reenie's Stuffed Zucchini

Renee Bayer—Gunnison, Colorado: "Great appetizer or meal!"

Zucchini 1 large
Rice 1 cup, cooked
Cheddar cheese 1/2 cup, shredded
Onion 1/2 cup, minced
Garlic powder 1/2 teaspoon
Seasoned salt 1/2 teaspoon
Pepper 1/2 teaspoon
Meat 1/2 cup, minced—ham, beef or chicken
Paprika
Red wine 1/3 cup

Cut zucchini crosswise into slices, 1 1/2 inches thick. Gently remove the center pulp and seeds. Place zucchini rings on a greased baking sheet. In a large bowl, thoroughly combine remaining ingredients, except paprika and wine. Spoon stuffing into each ring and garnish with paprika. Spoon a teaspoon of wine onto each ring. Bake at 375° for 20 minutes, until zucchini is tender. Spoon remaining wine over rings and bake 15 more minutes. Serves 6.

Tetrazzini Telluride Zucchini

Mo Mahoney—Telluride, Colorado: "I had to come up with lots of ways to eat the zucchini crawling in my backyard. This one's a favorite."

Zucchini 4 cups, diced
Salt 1/2 teaspoon
Pepper 1/2 teaspoon
Ham 2 1/4 cups, cooked and cut in strips
Mushroom 1 cup, sliced
Butter 1/3 cup

Onion 1/2 cup, chopped
Flour 1/3 cup
Chicken stock 1 cup, hot
Milk 1 1/4 cup
Swiss cheese 2/3 cup, shredded
Dry mustard 1/2 teaspoon
Parmesan 1/2 cup, grated

Steam zucchini until almost tender. Drain and sprinkle with salt and pepper. In a large pan, saute ham and mushrooms in butter. Remove ham and mushrooms and set aside. Saute onions in butter until golden. Sprinkle in flour and gently blend. Allow flour to cook slightly before gradually stirring in chicken stock and milk. Simmer and stir continuously until sauce thickens. Stir in cheese and mustard and continue stirring until cheese melts. Add ham, mushrooms and drained zucchini. Pour into a buttered casserole and sprinkle parmesan over the top. Broil until bubbly. Serves 6.

Sauteed and Cheesy Carrots and Zucchini

A tasty frittata that fits just as easily into brunch as it does dinner.

Zucchini 2 medium
Carrots 2 large
Garlic 2 cloves, crushed
Butter 3 tablespoons

Egg 1 beaten
Salt and pepper to taste
Cayenne to taste (optional)
Parmesan 1/3 cup, grated

Grate together zucchini and carrots. Saute garlic in butter. Add zucchini and carrots, stirring till tender. Quickly stir in egg. Add remaining ingredients and stir over low heat for 2 minutes. Sprinkle on more parmesan cheese just before serving. Serves 6-8.

Coconut-Curry Zucchini

Maureen Mahoney—Telluride, Colorado: "At potlucks, this dish is always the first one attacked."

Zucchini 2 cups, cubed
Onion 1/2 cup, minced
Garlic 1 large clove, crushed
Butter 3 tablespoons
Raisins 1/3 cup
Flour 2 tablespoons

Water 1 cup
Chicken bouillon 1 cube, crushed
Curry 1 teaspoon (or to taste)
Salt
Coconut 1/4 cup, shredded

Saute zucchini, onion and garlic in 1 tablespoon butter until almost tender. Remove to a warm dish and stir in raisins. Melt remaining butter and stir in flour. When golden, slowly stir in water with bouillon. Stir until sauce thickens. Add curry, salt and zucchini, and simmer 1 minute. Garnish with coconut. Serves 6.

A good eater must be a good man; for a good eater must have a good digestion, and a good digestion depends upon a good conscience.

—Benjamin Disraeli

Sour Cream and Dill Zucchini

Butter 1/2 cup
Zucchini 3 cups, thinly sliced
Dill 2 tablespoons fresh, chopped
Salt to taste

Pepper to taste
Sour cream 1 cup

Melt butter in saucepan over low heat. Stir in zucchini and saute for 1 minute. Sprinkle in dill, salt and pepper. Cook until tender. Gently stir in sour cream. Serves 6-8..

San Luis Calabacitas

"Calabacitas" is the Spanish word for "squash." This recipe gives summer squash--zucchini--a Mexican twist, thanks to green chiles, tomatoes, onions and plenty of cheese.

Zucchini 4 cups, diced
Vegetable oil 2 tablespoons
Onion 2/3 cup, diced
Tomatoes 3 large, chopped
Green chiles 5, cooked and
  chopped, or 1 large can

Salt to taste
Pepper to taste
Garlic powder 1/2 teaspoon
Cheese 1 cup, shredded,
  cheddar and jack

Steam zucchini until nearly tender and drain. Heat oil and saute onions until translucent. Add tomatoes, green chiles, salt, pepper and garlic powder, stirring well over low heat. Sprinkle in cheese and mix thoroughly until cheese melts. Continue to heat one minute.

The oldest continuously populated city in Colorado, San Luis was settled in 1851 by Mexicans. About 50 miles north of New Mexico, San Luis retains much of its Mexican heritage to this day.

Summer Squash Casserole

Yellow squash 3 cups, sliced
Onion 1 large, thinly sliced
Cream of mushroom soup 2 cans
Pepper 1/2 teaspoon
Dill 1/2 teaspoon

Water chestnuts 1 can, sliced
Sour cream 1 cup
Herb stuffing 1 cup
Butter 1/2 cup
Cheese 3/4 cup, grated

Steam squash and onions until tender. Mix in soup, pepper, dill, water chestnuts and sour cream. In a greased baking dish, spread half the stuffing to evenly cover bottom. Spoon squash on top. Cover with remaining stuffing. Drizzle on butter and sprinkle on grated cheese. Bake at 350° for 35 minutes, until cheese is bubbly.

Veggie Sesame

Broccoli 1 cup chopped
Cauliflower 1/2 cup, broken
  into florets
Onion 1 medium, chopped
Carrots 1 large, thinly sliced
Celery 1 large rib, chopped
Sesame oil 4 tablespoons

Vinegar 3 tablespoons
Sugar 3 tablespoons
Soy sauce 3 tablespoons
Water chestnuts 1 can, sliced
Bean sprouts 1/2 cup
Sesame seeds 4 tablespoons,
  toasted

Steam broccoli, cauliflower, onion, carrots and celery. Drain and transfer vegetables to serving bowl. In a saucepan, stir oil, vinegar, sugar and soy sauce over high heat to a boil. Mix water chestnuts and bean sprouts into steamed vegetables. Stir in sauce to coat evenly. Garnish with sesame seeds. Serves 4.

A cucumber should be well sliced and dressed with pepper and vinegar, and then thrown out, as good for nothing.
—Samuel Johnson

(Editor's note: Don't believe everything you read until trying the following recipe...)

Colorado Cucumbers au Gratin

Cucumbers 4 large, peeled, diced
Butter 1/4 cup
Flour 4 tablespoons
Salt and pepper to taste
Chicken stock 3/4 cup

Milk 2/3 cup
Egg yolks 3, well beaten
Nutmeg a dash
Bread crumbs 1 cup
Romano cheese 1/2 cup, grated

Boil cucumbers for 5 minutes. Drain. In a saucepan, melt butter and blend in salt and pepper. Add stock and milk, stirring until thick. Beat a small amount of hot sauce with egg yolks, then add it to remaining sauce. Add nutmeg and cucumbers. Pour into a greased casserole and cover with a mix of bread crumbs and cheese. Bake at 350° for 25 minutes, until golden and bubbly. Serves 6-8.

Ouray Cauliflower Souffle

A trip to Ouray is like stepping into Switzerland: Bavarian store fronts line the streets and outrageous peaks surround the entire town. This recipe turns cauliflower into a delicate, Swiss-cheese souffle.

Cauliflower 1 head, sliced or separated into florets
Onion 1/4 cup, diced
Salt 1/2 teaspoon
Pepper 1/2 teaspoon
Nutmeg 1/4 teaspoon
Cayenne a dash

Butter 1/4 cup
Flour 1/4 cup
Milk 1 1/2 cups, hot
Eggs 5
Swiss cheese 1 3/4 cup, grated
Bread crumbs 1/4 cup
Parsley 1/4 cup, fresh, chopped

Steam cauliflower and onion until tender. In a blender, puree cauliflower, onion, and spices. Melt butter and sprinkle in flour, cooking until slightly golden. Slowly add hot milk, stirring constantly until it thickens. Remove from stove. Add five egg yolks, one at a time, stirring well. Mix in cauliflower puree and 1 1/2 cups of cheese. Beat all egg whites with a pinch of salt until stiff and carefully fold into cauliflower. Pour into a buttered souffle dish, top with remaining cheese, bread crumbs and parsley. Bake at 400° for 40 minutes.

Sherry-Cream Mushrooms

Dawn Mailhot—Telluride, Colorado: "Great with wild mushrooms."

Mushrooms 1 pound, cleaned and sliced in thirds
Onions 1 medium, diced
Butter 1/2 cup
Flour 3 tablespoons
Parmesan 1/4 cup
Egg 1, beaten

Half-and-half 1/2 pint
Sherry 2 tablespoons
Salt and pepper to taste
Garlic powder 1/4 teaspoon
Cheese 2/3 cup, cheddar, grated
Bread crumbs 1 cup

Saute mushrooms and onions in butter. Stir in flour and parmesan. Spoon into a greased pan. Mix together egg, half-and-half, sherry and spices. Pour over mushrooms. Sprinkle on cheese and bread crumbs. Bake at 350° for 25 minutes, till cheese bubbles.

Eggplant Parmesan

An excellent main dish that both meat-eaters and vegetarians will enjoy. For an easy, inexpensive dinner party, serve with a tossed salad and a big loaf of Italian garlic bread.

Eggplant 1 large
Milk 2/3 cup
Eggs 2
Bread crumbs 1 1/2 cups
Garlic powder 3 teaspoons
Onion powder 2 teaspoons
Parmesan 1/2 cup, grated
Oil for frying
Tomato sauce 2 cups
Mozzarella cheese 1 lb., shredded

Slice eggplant to make 1/4-inch thick rounds. Beat together milk and eggs. In a large bowl, combine bread crumbs, garlic and onion powders, and 2 tablespoons parmesan. Dip eggplant into milk and egg mixture and then coat in bread crumbs. For thicker breading, dip back into milk and egg mixture and roll again in bread crumbs. Fry in hot oil until both sides are light golden. Drain on paper towels. Spread 3 tablespoons of tomato sauce in bottom of baking pan. Arrange eggplant in pan. Cover each with a heaping tablespoon of tomato sauce and mozzarella cheese. Sprinkle remaining parmesan over all. Bake at 350° for about 40 minutes, until mozzarella melts. Serves 4-6.

Veggie Kabobs

Experiment with different marinades and make room on the grill!

Cherry tomatoes
Onions cut in 1-inch chunks
Peppers green, red and yellow,
cut in 1/2-inch wide strips
Pineapple chunks 1 can
Zucchini 1/4-inch slices
Mushrooms
Cauliflower cut in florets

Carefully skewer vegetables, wrapping pepper strips around pineapple to secure. Season to taste and allow to marinate, if desired. Grill over a medium heat until cooked and slightly crisp. For softer vegetables, cook over simmering coals and cover grill.

Potato Patties

Carolyn Cotton—Brighton, Colorado: "We eat these with any leftover gravy--beef or chicken. They're delicious plain, too!"

Mashed potatoes 2 to 4 cups
Onion 1/4 cup, chopped
Salt 1 teaspoon

Pepper 1/4 teaspoon
Flour 2 tablespoons
Oil or shortening for frying

Mix together: potatoes, onion, salt, pepper and flour. Drop spoonfuls into skillet of hot oil, and smooth into patties (about 1/4 to 1/2 inch thick) with back of spoon. Fry each side until golden.

What I say is that, if a fellow really likes potatoes, he must be a decent sort of fellow.

— A.A. Milne

Baked Stuffed Potatoes

Andy Davis—Telluride, Colorado

Potatoes 4 large, Idaho style
Vegetable oil 2 tablespoons
Butter 1/4 cup
Sour cream 1/3 cup
Chives 2 tablespoons
Parmesan 1/4 cup, grated

Salt to taste
Pepper to taste
Paprika 1/2 teaspoon
Garlic powder 1/4 teaspoon
Onion powder 1/4 teaspoon
Butter 2 tablespoons, melted

Rub potatoes with vegetable oil and bake at 350° for 45 to 60 minutes, until pierced easily by a fork. Slice in halves and gently scoop out center. Whip potatoes with butter, sour cream, chives, cheese and spices. Spoon mixture into potato skins. Brush each with butter. Bake 10 to 15 minutes longer and serve.

Potatoes Alamosa

Potatoes 6 large, Idaho style
Onion 1/2 cup, chopped
Green chiles 1 (4 oz.) can, diced
Jalapenos 3 tablespoons, diced
Garlic powder

Onion powder
Cayenne to taste
Salt and pepper to taste
Cheese 3/4 cup, shredded, cheddar and jack
Milk enough to cover potatoes

Wash, peel and thinly slice potatoes. Arrange a layer of slices in a generously greased baking dish. Sprinkle on two tablespoons of onion, one-third of the chiles and jalapenos. Shake on garlic and onion powders, cayenne, salt and pepper--to taste. Spread one-third of the cheese on top. Add two more layers of potatoes and remaining ingredients. Pour on enough milk to cover. Bake at 375° for 30 minutes. Remove cover and continue to bake until top turns golden brown--about 15 minutes. Serves 8.

Meaning "cottonwood grove" in Spanish, Alamosa owes much of its livelihood to irrigation, which was introduced in the 1880s. The canals turned this Rio Grande valley into a fertile farmland especially suited for growing potatoes.

Southwestern Potato Pie

Mushrooms 1 1/2 cups, sliced
Onion 1/3 cup, minced
Butter 2 tablespoons
Lemon juice 1 teaspoon
Salt 1/2 teaspoon

Pepper to taste
Paprika to taste
Cayenne to taste
Potatoes 3 cups, mashed
Sour cream 1/2 cup

Saute mushrooms and onions in butter until onions are translucent. Add lemon juice and spices. Mix well. Smooth half the mashed potatoes evenly in the bottom of a buttered pie plate. Top with sour cream and mushroom mixture. Cover with remaining potatoes. Bake at 350° for 40 minutes. Slice in wedges and serve.

Sweet Potato Crisp

Courtesy of Waunita Hot Springs Ranch—Gunnison, Colorado

Sweet potatoes 7 cups, cooked and mashed
Sugar 3/4 cup
Margarine 3/4 cup
Eggs 2
Milk 1/3 cup

Vanilla 1 teaspoon
Brown sugar 3/4 cup, light
Flour 1/2 cup
Margarine 3/4 cup, melted
Pecans 3/4 cup, chopped

Blend sweet potatoes, sugar, margarine, eggs, milk and vanilla until creamy. Combine brown sugar and flour. Add 3/4 cup melted margarine and pecans. Place sweet potato mixture in large casserole. Cover with brown sugar mixture. Bake at 350° for 30 minutes or until thoroughly heated. Serves 10.

Scallop of White Winter Vegetables

Lee Schillereff—Canon City, Colorado

Potatoes 3 medium
Turnips 3 small
Parsnips 3 small
Fennel bulb 1
Cauliflower optional
White cabbage optional

Green onions 1 bunch, thinly sliced, white part only
Celery 1/2 cup, diced, inner stalks
Ranch dressing 1 1/2 to 2 cups, made with buttermilk
Fennel leaves for garnish

Peel and/or cut first 6 vegetables and steam them until tender in a covered saucepan. Drain. Add green onions and raw celery. Drizzle with ranch dressing. Pour into casserole coated with non-stick spray, and cover. Bake at 350° for about 20 minutes. Garnish with feathery fennel leaves before serving. Serves 6.

Breads, Rolls and Muffins

Bread may be the staff of life, but as these recipes prove, it can be passion for the tastebuds. To this chapter we bring its many variations: from sweet rolls, flavorful muffins and decadent loaves, to Southwestern savories and a Native American recipe that's as old as the hills. . .

McGraw Cinnamon Rolls

Guests of McGraw Ranch in Estes Park rave about Ruth McGraw 's cinnamon rolls --a filling snack and sweet breakfast treat.

Yeast 3 cakes
Eggs 2
Water 1 cup, lukewarm
Sugar 1/2 cup
Salt 2 teaspoons
Shortening 1/2 cup
Water 4 cups, boiling
Raisins 1 cup, golden
Walnuts 1 cup, finely chopped
Flour about 5 pounds

Brown sugar 2 pounds
Oleo 3/4 pound, melted
Cinnamon 12 tablespoons

Frosting:
Canned milk 1/2 cup
Vanilla 1 tablespoon
Oleo 1 cup, browned
Powdered sugar 3 cups

Beat yeast, eggs and lukewarm water until foamy. In a separate bowl, mix together 1/2 cup sugar, salt and 1/2 cup shortening. Pour four cups of boiling water over this mixture and set aside to cool. Add raisins and walnuts to the yeast mixture. Add enough flour to make a soft dough. Kneed and let dough rise once. Form it into a round ball. Combine brown sugar, 3/4 pound melted oleo and cinnamon. Roll dough to 1/2 inch thickness. Spread brown sugar mixture evenly over dough. Roll and cut into slices--1 1/2 inches thick. Place slices on greased baking sheet about 3 inches apart. Let rise for 20 minutes. Bake in a preheated oven at 300° for 30 minutes.

For frosting: combine canned milk, vanilla, one cup of browned and cooled oleo and powdered sugar. Beat or stir until smooth. Drizzle the frosting over rolls once they are removed from the oven.

NOTE: This recipe makes enough to feed the whole ranch!

Sweet Dinner Rolls

Sharon Galligar Chance—Colorado Springs, Colorado

Eggs 3
Sugar 1 cup
Shortening 1 cup
Water 2 cups

Salt 2 teaspoons
Yeast 2 packages
Water 1/2 cup, warm
Flour 9 cups

Beat together eggs and sugar. Blend in shortening, two cups water and salt. Dissolve yeast in warm water and add to egg mixture. Mix in four cups flour. Add remaining flour, one cup at a time. Set aside to rise. Once the dough has risen, knead well and pinch out rolls. Place on well-greased cookie sheets and set aside to rise again. Bake in a preheated oven at 450° for 10 minutes.

Poppy Seed Poundcake Muffins

Thanks to Judy Clemmer, the smell of these delicate muffins baking in the oven fills every corner of the Leadville Country Inn, a well-respected restaurant in Colorado's high country.

Sugar 1 cup
Butter 1/2 cup
Eggs 2, beaten
Yogurt 1 cup, plain
Vanilla 1 teaspoon (or almond
    extract may be used)

Flour 2 cups
Baking soda 1/4 teaspoon
Salt 1/2 teaspoon
Poppy seeds 3 teaspoons

Cream together sugar, butter and beaten eggs. Beat in yogurt and add flavoring. Combine flour, baking soda, salt and poppy seeds. Stir into creamed mixture. Pour batter into well-greased muffin tins. Bake in a preheated oven at 400° for 15 to 20 minutes, or until golden brown.

The Hearthstone Inn's Chocolate Bread with Vanilla Butter

Once featured in America West magazine, this recipe has earned Colorado Springs' innkeepers Dot and Ruth Williams high praise. "The yeasty-chocolaty smell will bring people in off the street," says Dot. Considered one of Colorado's premiere B&Bs, the Hearthstone Inn has all the charm of a country hideaway, the elegance of a Victorian inn, all the comforts of home, as well as glorious views of Pikes Peak. The food? Recipes such as this one speak for themselves.

Milk 1 cup
Butter 2 tablespoons
Sugar 1/2 cup
Vanilla 1 teaspoon
Yeast 1 package
Eggs 2, beaten
Flour 3 1/2 cups
Cocoa 2/3 cup

Walnuts 1 cup, chopped
  (optional)
Sugar 1 tablespoon

Vanilla Butter:
Butter 12 tablespoons
Powdered sugar 3/4 cup
Vanilla 2 tablespoons

Scald milk and remove from heat. Add butter, stirring until it melts. Add 1/2 cup sugar and vanilla. Dissolve yeast in 1/4 cup tepid water mixed with 1 tablespoon sugar. After yeast is good and frothy, add it to cooled milk mixture. Stir in beaten eggs. Measure flour and cocoa into a large bowl. Add nuts, if desired. Add milk-and-egg mixture and stir vigorously. Turn out onto a floured board. Knead dough for 5 minutes, adding more flour if necessary. Place into greased bowl, cover and let rise for 1 1/2 hours. Punch down and let rise again. (Dough only needs to rise twice if being prepared at elevations over 6,500 feet.) Knead dough 10 times. Shape, place in 9 x 5 pan and allow to rise another 30 minutes. Put sugar on top of the loaf. Bake in a preheated oven at 350° for 30 minutes or until loaf sounds hollow when tapped. Cool 10 minutes in pan. Serve with Vanilla Butter. To prepare butter, cream together all ingredients until smooth and fluffy.

Fresh Dill Bread

Lovingly prepared at The Prospector Restaurant in Leadville, Colorado, where all breads are served fresh. "This recipe is a favorite, made from fresh dill, which is always available from the gardens of friends and customers."

Yeast 1 package, "fast" type
Sugar 2 tablespoons
Water 1 1/2 cups, warm
Water 1 1/2 cups, hot
Butter 1/2 cup
Salt 1 tablespoon

Cottage cheese 3/4 cup
Dry minced onion 1 tablespoon
Fresh dill 1/2 cup, minced, or
  substitute 1/4 cup dry dill
Flour 4 to 8 cups
Butter 2 tablespoons, melted

Mix together yeast, sugar and warm water. Set aside in a warm place to activate the yeast. In a saucepan over high heat, mix remaining water, butter, salt, cottage cheese, minced onion and dill. Heat until butter melts. Pour into mixer and beat in three cups of flour. Add yeast mixture. Beat in enough flour to make dough fairly stiff, elastic and unsticky. Form into one or two loaves. Brush with melted butter and bake in a preheated oven at 350° for about 25 minutes.

Buttermilk Biscuits

Flour 2 cups
Salt 1 teaspoon
Baking soda 1/2 teaspoon

Baking powder 1 teaspoon
Butter 3 tablespoons
Buttermilk 1 cup

Combine flour, salt, baking soda and baking powder. Cut in butter and work it until coarse in texture. Gradually stir in buttermilk, adding only enough to make a soft dough. On a floured surface, roll the dough out to 1/2 inch thickness. Cut out with a floured biscuit cutter. Bake in a preheated oven at 400° for about 12 minutes, or until biscuits are golden brown. Serve immediately, plain, or with butter, honey or jam.

Currant Scones

Flour 1 cup
Baking soda 1/2 teaspoon
Salt one good pinch
Cream of tartar 1 teaspoon

Butter 2 tablespoons, melted
Currants 1/4 cup
Milk 1/4 pint

Sift together flour, baking soda, salt and cream of tartar. Run in the butter lightly and add the currants. Form a well in the mixture and add sufficient milk to form a spongy, dry dough. Knead gently for a moment, place on a floured board and lightly roll out to about 3/4 inch thick. Cut into rounds, arrange on a floured tray and bake in a preheated oven at 450° for about 10 minutes.

As British as the Beatles, scones came to Colorado by way of the Cornish men and women who left their homeland to work the mines and farms of the Rocky Mountain state. The Cornish scone recipes presented here are courtesy of the Gilpin Historical Society of Central City, Colorado.

Oatmeal Scones

Flour 3/4 cup
Salt one good pinch
Baking soda 1/2 teaspoon
Cream of tartar 1/2 teaspoon

Butter 2 tablespoons
Oatmeal 1/4 cup
Milk

Sift together flour, salt, baking soda and cream of tartar. Rub in butter with fingertips. Mix in oatmeal. Make a well in the center of the dough and gradually add enough milk to form a soft and spongy dough that is not sticky. Quickly and lightly roll out on a floured board to about one inch thickness. Cut into rounds, place on a floured baking tray and bake in a preheated oven at 450° for about 8 minutes.

Panocha

Amelia V. Smith—Pueblo, Colorado: "This 'pudding' is served during the Lenten season and is very nourishing. It may be stored in a tight container in the refrigerator."

Sprouted wheat flour 2 cups
Wheat flour 1 cup
Boiling water 4 cups
Sugar 1 cup

Butter 3 tablespoons
Cloves 1/8 teaspoon
Cinnamon 1/4 teaspoon

Sift flours well and combine with two cups boiling water and 1/2 cup sugar. Stir quickly to avoid lumping. Add butter; stir well and set aside. In a heavy saucepan, caramelize remaining sugar. Add two cups boiling water to "burnt" sugar. Blend into flour mixture and add spices. Pour into a well-buttered two-quart casserole. Bake in a preheated oven uncovered at 375° for one hour. Pudding will be thick and dark brown. Serve plain or with cream or milk.

Carob Chip Muffins

Innkeeper Sallie Clark has a reputation for serving extraordinary breakfasts at Colorado Springs' Holden House 1902. For some of her personal favorites, turn to 'Breakfasts and Brunch' recipes.

Egg 1, slightly beaten
Butter 1/3 cup, softened
Milk 1/2 cup
Sour cream 1/2 cup
Flour 2 1/2 cups
Baking powder 1 tablespoon

Sugar 1/3 cup
Brown sugar 1/3 cup
Salt 1 pinch
Carob chips 1 cup
Walnuts 1/2 cup, chopped
Honey 2 tablespoons

Cream together egg, butter, milk and sour cream. In separate bowl, combine flour, baking powder, sugars, and salt. Add to egg mixture and combine thoroughly. Add carob chips. Pour into greased muffin tins, top with walnuts and a teaspoon of honey. Bake in a preheated oven at 400° for 25 to 30 minutes, until lightly browned.

Mexicali Corn Muffins

Cornmeal 2/3 cup
Flour 1 1/3 cups
Sugar 2 tablespoons
Salt 1/2 teaspoon
Cayenne 1/4 teaspoon
Baking powder 4 teaspoons
Milk 3/4 cup

Sour cream 1/3 cup
Oil 1/4 cup
Egg 1 beaten
Green chiles 1 (4 oz.) can, chopped
Cheddar cheese 1/2 cup, grated
Onion 1 small, minced

Combine together: cornmeal, flour, sugar, salt, cayenne and baking powder in a large bowl. In a separate bowl, mix milk, sour cream, oil and egg. Add to dry ingredients, along with green chiles, cheese and onion. Mix just until moistened, being careful not to overmix. Fill greased muffin tins 2/3 full. Bake in a preheated oven at 375° for about 20 minutes or until golden brown. Turn out of pan onto a cooling rack immediately.

When I am in trouble, eating is the only thing that consoles me... At the present moment I am eating muffins because I am unhappy. Besides, I am particularly fond of muffins.

From "The Importance of Being Earnest," by Oscar Wilde

Buttermilk Huckleberry Muffins

If huckleberries are out of reach, substitute fresh blueberries.

Flour 2 cups
Baking soda 1/4 teaspoon
Baking powder 1 tablespoon
Salt 3/4 teaspoon
Sugar 1/2 cup

Vegetable oil 1/3 cup
Eggs 2, beaten
Buttermilk 1 1/2 cups
Huckleberries 1 1/2 cups, rinsed and patted dry

Sift together flour, baking soda and baking powder, salt and sugar. Blend oil, eggs and buttermilk till smooth. Add to dry ingredients and mix thoroughly. Gently fold in huckleberries. Pour into greased muffin tins. Bake in a preheated oven at 375° for 25 to 30 minutes, or until golden brown. Makes 2 dozen.

Southwestern Corn Popovers

Light and cheesy, with a bit of a kick from jalapenos and cayenne.

Corn 1 2/3 cup, kernels
Milk 1/4 cup
Eggs 2
Flour 1 cup
Baking powder 1/4 teaspoon
Sugar 1 teaspoon
Salt 1/2 teaspoon

White pepper 1/2 teaspoon
Cayenne 1/4 teaspoon
Crushed red pepper
  1/4 teaspoon
Jalapeno 1 medium
Jack cheese 1/4 cup, grated

Puree corn with 1/4 cup milk in an electric blender. Pour puree into bowl. Strain all juices from the puree back into blender and discard kernel remains. Add remaining ingredients and blend until completely smooth. Let batter rest about 1 hour. Grease popover pans thoroughly and place in a preheated 450° oven for 2 minutes before pouring in batter. Fill pans until 2/3 full and bake 15 minutes. Reduce heat to 375° and bake an additional 10 to 15 minutes until light brown. Serve immediately.

Native American Bread

An adaptation of American Indian fry bread, this version may be served in a variety of ways: cut in triangles and served with salsa or other dipping condiments; folded over and stuffed like a taco; or topped with refried beans, cheese, shredded lettuce and tomatoes-- for an Indian-Mexican style tostada. Experiment and enjoy.

Flour 5 cups
Salt 1 teaspoon
Baking powder 2 tablespoons

Butter 1 tablespoon
Milk 2 cups
Vegetable oil for frying

Sift 4 cups of flour with salt and baking powder. In a saucepan, melt butter, cool slightly and add milk. Add milk mixture a little at a time to flour, stirring well after each addition. Work into a soft dough. Turn onto floured surface, kneading and working in remaining flour. Divide dough into 6 equal balls. Flatten until about 1/8th inch thick and drop into very hot oil. Brown on both sides.

Desserts

It was 1892... the mining industry was sinking like a sack of potatoes. But just before hitting rock bottom, Coloradans "sweetened" their economy... literally. That year, a Sugar Convention prompted the Denver Chamber of Commerce to distribute sugar-beet seeds to local farmers as incentive to promote a new agricultural industry. And it paid off: The Colorado Sugar Manufacturing Company opened the state's first sugar-beet factory in 1899. And, within a few years others began popping up around the region: in Rocky Ford, Sugar City, Loveland, Fort Collins, Longmont and Windsor. The high altitude, cool weather and controlled irrigation yielded a crop that placed Colorado's sugar-beet industry in top ranks nationwide. Celebrating the birth of this "sweet" industry, we'd like to share some of Colorado's favorite dessert recipes...

High Country Rum Cake

Barbara A. Sabol—Cascade, Colorado: "A moist, wonderful cake."

Cake mix 1 package
Pudding mix 1 small package
Rum 1/2 cup
Water 1/2 cup
Vegetable oil 1/2 cup
Eggs 4

Glaze:
Margarine 1/2 cup
Water 1/4 cup
Rum 1/4 cup
Sugar 1 cup

Blend cake ingredients and pour into bundt pan. Bake in a preheated oven at 350° for 45 minutes or until a toothpick inserted in center comes out clean. During the last 10 minutes of baking time, bring the glaze ingredients to a boil for one minute. Pour over cake immediately after it is removed from oven. Cool 15 minutes before removing from pan. (The cake will fall apart if removed from pan too early.)

Suggested cake and pudding combinations: yellow cake and pistachio pudding; chocolate cake and chocolate/vanilla pudding; yellow cake and banana pudding; banana cake and banana pudding; butter-pecan cake and vanilla pudding; strawberry cake and vanilla pudding; white or yellow cake and butterscotch pudding.

Rawah Ranch
Sour Cream Pound Cake

An old favorite at Rawah Ranch in Glendevey, this recipe first appeared in "Favorite Ranch Recipes," a collaborative cookbook published by the Colorado Dude and Guest Ranch Association.

Butter 1 cup
Sugar 2 1/2 cups
Eggs 6
Flour 3 cups, sifted
Salt 1/2 teaspoon

Baking soda 1/2 teaspoon
Sour cream 1 cup
Vanilla 1/2 teaspoon
Lemon extract 1/2 teaspoon
Orange extract 1/2 teaspoon

Cream butter and sugar until light and fluffy. Add eggs, one at a time, beating well. Sift together flour, salt and baking soda. Add dry ingredients alternately with sour cream to the butter mixture and beat until smooth. Add extracts. Spoon batter into an ungreased nine-inch tube pan lined with waxed paper on the bottom. Bake in a preheated oven at 350° for 1 hour and 15 minutes, or until toothpick comes clean after being inserted into center of cake. Cool for about 10 minutes, gently loosen with a spatula and flip onto serving plate. Carefully peel off the paper. Cool thoroughly before slicing. (Notes: Like most pound cakes, this will not rise to the top of pan. Also, recipe may need adjustments for high-altitude baking.)

Peach Upside Down Cake

Georgia aside, there's nothing like a fresh Colorado peach.

Butter 1/2 cup
Brown sugar 1 cup, light

Peaches 5 cups, sliced
Yellow cake mix 1 package

As oven preheats to 350°, melt 1/4 cup butter in two 9-inch round cake pans. Remove from oven. Sprinkle 1/2 cup of brown sugar into each pan and arrange peach slices to cover. Follow the package directions to prepare cake mix. Pour batter into peach-lined cake pans and bake 25-35 minutes or until done. Cool for 5 minutes and invert onto serving plate.

Dianne's Spicy Ski Cake

After a day of pushing around powder on Telluride's slopes, guests of the San Sophia Bed & Breakfast Inn fall back onto plush sofas and, if they're lucky, savor a slice of this spicy, chocolate-nut cake.

Flour 3 cups
Baking soda 1 1/2 teaspoons
Cinnamon 1 1/2 teaspoons
Salt 1 teaspoon
Nutmeg 3/4 teaspoon
Cloves 1/4 teaspoon, ground
Pecans 1 1/2 cups
Sugar 1 3/4 cups

Butter or margarine 3/4 cup,
at room temperature
Eggs 3
Applesauce 1 1/2 cups
Semisweet chocolate chips
1 (12 oz.) bag
Powder sugar 2 tablespoons

In a large bowl, combine first 6 ingredients and set aside. Chop pecans. In a large mixing bowl, cream sugar and butter until light and fluffy, frequently scraping sides of bowl. Add eggs, one at a time, beating well after each addition. Reduce mixing speed to low. Add flour mixture, alternating with applesauce, and beat until smooth. Fold in1 cup each of chocolate chips and pecan pieces. Pour batter into greased and floured tube or bundt pan. Sprinkle remaining chips and nuts on top. Bake in a preheated oven at 350° for one hour, or until toothpick inserted into center comes out clean. Cool 20 minutes on wire rack, loosen edges with knife, turn cake over onto rack and let cool completely. Dust top of cake with powdered sugar.

Popcorn Cake

If the recipe title didn't make you do a double take, the cake certainly will. This unusual treat is the creation of Junelle Pringle of Gunnison.

Margarine 1/2 cup
Marshmallows 14 ounces
Popcorn 3 quarts, popped

Virginia peanuts 1 cup
M & M's 1 cup (optional)

Melt margarine and marshmallows in double boiler. Stir until marshmallows dissolve and cool slightly. Pour over popcorn, nuts and M&M's. Mix well. Turn into greased tube pan, and smooth. Unmold immediately. Cool well before slicing. Serves 14.

Carrot Cake

Violet Hale—Manitou Springs, Colorado: "May be frozen for up to three months and then thawed before serving."

Salad oil 1 cup
Sugar 2 cups
Eggs 4
Flour 2 cups
Soda 1 teaspoon

Cinnamon 1 teaspoon
Salt 1/4 teaspoon
Vanilla 1 teaspoon
Carrots 3 cups, grated
Nuts 1 cup, chopped

Cream oil and sugar together. Add eggs and beat well. Mix together the dry ingredients and add to sugar mixture. Blend in carrots and nuts. Pour into a greased and floured 9 x13 pan and bake in a preheated oven at 375° for 40-45 minutes. May be served plain or with cream cheese frosting.

> *Built in 1895, Miramont Castle boasts nine architectural styles, from Byzantine to Romanesque. Nearby are the Manitou Hot Springs, believed to have mystical healing powers. The recipes here represent the decadent offerings of the castle's Tea Room, open year-round.*

Castle Cheesecake

Violet Hale—Manitou Springs, Colorado: "Another one that can be made ahead, frozen and then thawed completely before serving."

Eggs 1 whole, 1 yolk
Lemon juice from 1/2 lemon
Butter 1 1/4 cups
Flour 2 cups
Cream cheese 4 (8 oz.) packages
Sour cream 1 cup

Sugar 1 1/2 cups
Vanilla 1 tablespoon
Eggs 4
Egg whites 4, whipped
Lemon juice from 1 lemon

Mix first four ingredients to make crust. Form in springform 12" pan and place in freezer. Mix together remaining ingredients and beat well. Take crust from freezer and pour in filling. Bake in a preheated oven at 350° for 30-40 minutes. Cool before serving. Refrigerate leftovers.

Butter Pecan Rum Cake

Patrons of the Ore House restaurant in Durango, Colorado, know this unforgettable cake by its pseudonym--Ore House Rum Cake. Created by Sharon Abshagen, who co-owns the Ore House with her husband Bill (a.k.a. "Beatle"), this cake was named The Grand Champion of Show in the 1991 La Plata County Fair baking competition.

Pecans or walnuts 1 cup
Butter pecan cake mix 1 package
**Jello® vanilla pudding and pie
   filling** 3 1/2 ounce package
Eggs 4
Water 1/2 cup, cold
Oil 1/2 cup

Bacardi®dark rum 1/2 cup

Glaze:
Butter 1/3 cup
Water 1/3 cup
Bacardi®dark rum 1/3 cup
Sugar 1 1/4 cup

Preheat oven to 325°. Grease and flour 10-inch tube or 12-cup bundt pan. Sprinkle nuts in bottom of pan. Mix all cake ingredients together. Pour batter over nuts. Bake in a preheated oven 1 hour. For glaze, melt butter and stir in remaining ingredients. Allow mixture to come to a boil over medium heat. Turn off and let set. When cake is removed from oven, pour glaze over the top--leaving cake in pan. Let set for 30 minutes. Invert cake on serving plate.

Cornish Caraway Cake

Many of the gold miners in Central City, Colorado originated from Cornwall, England. With them, came many recipes of the homeland, such as this one. (Courtesy of the Gilpin County Historical Society.)

Sugar 1/2 cup
Butter 1/2 cup
Eggs 2
Flour 3/4 cup

Baking powder 1/2 teaspoon
Salt dash
Caraway seeds 1 teaspoon
Milk as needed

Cream butter and sugar. Add eggs, beating well after each. Sift together flour, baking powder and salt. Mix in seeds. Fold into the butter mixture, and add enough milk so that batter drops off a spoon. Bake in a preheated oven at 400° for about one hour.

Winding River Oatmeal Cake

Looking for an excuse to eat cake for breakfast? Try this one with oats and brown sugar. First published in "Favorite Ranch Recipes," a collaborative cookbook published by the Colorado Dude and Guest Ranch Association, this easy-to-prepare recipe comes by way of Winding River Ranch in Grand Lake, Colorado.

Water 1 1/2 cups
Oatmeal 1 cup
Raw sugar 1 cup
Shortening 1/2 cup
Sea salt 1/2 teaspoon
Eggs 2
Brown sugar 1/2 cup
Cinnamon 1 teaspoon

Baking Soda 1 teaspoon
Flour 1 1/2 cups, stone ground
Frosting:
Butter 1 cup
Brown sugar 1/2 cup
Flour 1/2 cup
Coconut 1 cup

Pour boiling water over oatmeal and set aside for 10 minutes. Add remaining cake ingredients and mix thoroughly. Pour into greased cake pan and bake in a preheated oven at 350° until toothpick inserted in center comes out clean. Cool completely. For frosting, cream butter and sugar. Mix in flour. Stir in coconut and frost cooled cake.

Oatmeal Peanut Butter Cookies

Mrs. Merle Hall—Springfield, Colorado: "My husband's favorite cookie!"

Margarine 1/2 cup
Brown sugar 3/4 cup
Sugar 3/4 cup
Vanilla 1 teaspoon
Eggs 3
Peanut butter 2 1/4 cups
Flour 1/2 cup
Oats 4 cups, raw

Baking soda 1 teaspoon
Salt 1 teaspoon
Coconut flakes 1 cup
Nuts 3/4 cup, chopped
Chocolate chips 1/2 cup
Butterscotch chips 1/2 cup
Raisins 1/2 cup

In large bowl, mix together margarine, sugars, vanilla, eggs and peanut butter. Beat until well-blended. Mix flour, oats, soda and salt together, and add to first mixture. Mix in remaining ingredients. Drop by heaping teaspoonfuls on lightly greased cookie sheets. Bake in a preheated oven at 375° for 15 minutes or lightly browned.

Delightful Strawberry Tidbits

Sharon Galligar Chance—Colorado Springs, Colorado: "Kids love to help make these. They are beautiful for Christmas."

Jello® 2 small boxes,
  wild strawberry flavor
Eagle Brand® sweetened
  condensed milk 3/4 cup

Coconut 1 cup
Nuts 1/2 cup, chopped
Sugar dyed red and green

Mix together the first four ingredients. Allow to cool in refrigerator for about two hours. Shape mixture into conical shapes that resemble strawberries. Roll in red sugar, then dip large end into green sugar for stem and leaves.

As sure as there are strawberries, Glenwood Springs celebrates Strawberry Days, one of the oldest annual events in the state. It started on one mid-June day in 1898 with free strawberries and ice cream.

These days, festivalgoers saddle up for pony-express rides, kick up their heels to live Western music, and kick up a storm during running and mountain-bike races. Fortunately, some things never change... the strawberries and ice cream are still free for the taking.

Strawberry Cooler Cake

Strawberries 1 1/2 cups
Sugar 3/4 cup
Lemon juice 1 tablespoon
Graham crackers 3 cups, crushed

Heavy cream 1/2 cup
Vanilla 1 1/2 teaspoons
Whipped cream for garnish
Strawberries halves, for garnish

In a large bowl, crush strawberries. Add sugar, lemon juice, graham-cracker crumbs, cream and vanilla. Mix well. Line a freezer tray with waxed paper. Pour in batter and freeze 2 hours, or until solid. Remove from tray and cut into squares. Garnish each piece with a dollop of whipped cream and a half strawberry.

Prospector Chocolate Mousse

An elegant dessert prepared at The Prospector Restaurant in Leadville.

Baking chocolate or chocolate chips 6 ounces, melted
Whipping cream 1 pint, unwhipped
Salt pinch

Egg yolks 3 large
Almond extract 1/2 teaspoon
Whipping cream 1 pint, whipped until stiff

In a heavy saucepan or double boiler, heat the chocolate, unwhipped cream and salt, stirring constantly. Add yolks and stir until well blended. Heat to a boil, stirring constantly. Remove from heat and stir in almond extract. Cool to room temperature. Gently fold in whipped cream. Spoon lightly into tall glasses and garnish with more whipped cream.

Chickie's Saucepan Brownies

Carolyn Cotton—Brighton, Colorado: "These are good and quick."

Margarine 1 cup
Eggs 4
Sugar 2 cups
Flour 2 cups
Cocoa 4 heaping tablespoons
Vanilla 2 teaspoons
Salt 1/2 teaspoon
Baking powder 2 teaspoons
Walnuts 1 cup, chopped (optional)

Glaze:
Cocoa 3 tablespoons
Margarine 3 tablespoons
Powdered sugar 1 1/2 cups
Vanilla 1 teaspoon
Water 3 tablespoons, boiling

Melt margarine in heavy pan. Turn off heat and blend in rest of ingredients. Spread batter in a greased and floured jelly-roll pan (or two 9x13 baking pans). Bake in a preheated oven at 350° for 15 minutes. While brownies are baking, melt margarine and cocoa over low heat. Stir in powdered sugar and vanilla. Add water, one tablespoon at a time, and stir till smooth. If needed, add a little more water to make the glaze fairly thin. Pour glaze over brownies immediately after they are removed from the oven.

Hello Dolly's

The ultimate dessert bar, 'Dolly's' come by way of the "Favorite Ranch Recipes" cookbook, that admittedly "stole" the recipe from Ruth McGraw, owner of McGraw Ranch in Estes Park, Colorado.

Butter 1/2 cup
Graham cracker crumbs 1 cup
Chocolate chips 1 cup or 1
   6-ounce package
Butterscotch morsels
   6-ounce package

Coconut 1 cup
Nuts 1/2 cup, chopped
   (sliced almonds)
Eagle Brand®sweetened
   condensed milk 1 can

Melt butter in 8x12 pan. Put graham cracker crumbs evenly over butter. Sprinkle in rest of ingredients in order given. Pour milk over all. Sprinkle on nuts. Bake in a preheated oven at 350° for 30 minutes. Cook in pan 15 minutes before cutting into squares.

Cowboy Cookies

Butter 1 cup, room temperature
Sugar 3/4 cup
Brown sugar 3/4 cup, packed
Eggs 2
Vanilla 1 1/2 teaspoons
Flour 2 cups

Baking soda 1 teaspoon
Baking powder 1/2 teaspoon
Salt 1 teaspoon
Chocolate chips 1 cup
Oats 3/4 cup
Nuts 3/4 cup, chopped

Cream together butter and sugars. Add eggs and vanilla; beat well. In separate bowl, sift together flour, baking soda, baking powder and salt. Add a little bit at a time to the butter mixture, stirring well. When thoroughly combined and smooth, stir in chocolate chips, oats and nuts. Drop big spoonfuls (cowboys like their cookies very large in size) onto a lightly greased cookie sheet. Bake in a preheated oven at 350° for about 15 minutes, until lightly browned. These may be frozen and thawed within minutes. Hide some away. They go fast!

Colorado Peach Dumplings

Barbara Sabol—Cascade, Colorado: "These dumplings are absolutely delicious! Peaches from Colorado's western slope are large, juicy and have a heavenly flavor. When peaches are out of season, canned peach halves may be used. Dumplings also freeze well."

Flour 4 cups
Shortening 1 1/2 cups
Almond extract 1/2 teaspoon
Water 2 cups, ice cold
Peaches 6 whole, peeled and pitted

Cinnamon glaze:
Water 1 cup
Sugar 3/4 cup
Cinnamon 2 tablespoons

Cut together flour, shortening, almond extract. Add just enough water to make dough workable. Roll out to 1/4-inch thick on a floured surface and cut into 6-inch squares. Place a peach in the center of each square and sprinkle with 2 tablespoons sugar. Pull up each corner of dough and wrap over peach, wetting the last corner to seal the dumpling. Place in baking dish sprayed with non-stick coating. Bake in a preheated oven at 375° for 20 minutes. For glaze, boil the ingredients together for about 3 minutes. Pour over dumplings and return them to oven. Continue baking for 10 minutes. Makes six dumplings.

The northwest region of Colorado, now referred to as the Western Slope, was Colorado's last frontier. First known to trappers and cattle rustlers, the region took a turn toward agricultural farming in the late 1800s. Once likened to the Sahara Desert, the area became the state's fruit basket, and eventually earned a reputation nationwide for growing fine fruit varieties. On top of the list for quality are the Western Slope peaches. The largest city in the region, Grand Junction, inaugurated its first Peach Day in 1891, a celebration that earned an annual August date on the calendar and continues to do so to this day.

Rawah Ranch Peach Cobbler

A dude ranch since 1950, Rawah Ranch rests in a secluded valley on the Laramie River in northern Colorado. When preparing this dessert, ranch owner and baker Ardy Kunz suggests using fresh or fresh-frozen peaches. Once the pie leaves the oven, she advises: "Cool slightly, serve with vanilla ice cream and invite me over for dessert!"

Sliced peaches 2 cups
Sugar 1/2 cup
Butter 1/2 cup
Flour 1 cup

Baking powder 1 1/2 teaspoons
Salt 1/2 teaspoon
Milk 1 cup
Sugar 1 cup

Mix peaches with sugar and set aside for about an hour. Melt butter in a 9x12 pan in oven. Mix together flour and baking powder. In a separate bowl, beat together milk and sugar. Combine flour and sugar mixture thoroughly. Pour into buttered pan. Spread peaches over batter. Bake in a preheated oven at 350° for 30 minutes, until brown and bubbly. Note: For elevations over 6,000 feet, use only 1 1/4 teaspoons baking powder and 3/4 cup sugar, but increase milk to 1 1/4 cups.

On the Western slope, among the peach orchards of Palisade, the locals celebrate the August harvest during the annual Palisade Peach Festival. Featured events include a parade, bands, arts, crafts, talent show, dance and food, food, food.

Native American Pudding

An age-old recipe that's even more American than apple pie. Delicious by itself or topped with heavy cream or vanilla ice cream.

Cornmeal 1 1/2 cups
Molasses 2/3 cup, black
Butter 1/3 cup
Sugar 1/3 cup

Salt 1/4 teaspoon
Baking soda 1/2 teaspoon
Eggs 3
Milk 9 cups

In a large saucepan, thoroughly mix all the ingredients except milk. Stir in five cups of hot milk. Allow to simmer for 30 minutes, until mixture boils. Stir in remaining milk. Pour into a well-greased casserole pan. Bake in a preheated oven at 275° until pudding is firm and golden.

In La Junta in June, interpreters of Native American history create an 1840 Indian Encampment, recreating an Indian camp in a cottonwood grove near Bent's Old Fort. And come August, the town of Beulah comes alive with the Paradise Valley Pow-Wow, featuring ceremonial dancing and portrayal of traditional Indian customs. Not to be missed at the pow-wow are the Native American food, crafts and jewelry.

Bread Pudding

Bread cubes 2 cups
Brown sugar 1/2 cup
Salt 1/2 teaspoon
Cinnamon 1 teaspoon
Vanilla 1 teaspoon

Milk 2 1/2 cups
Raisins 1/2 cup
Eggs 2, beaten lightly
Walnuts 1/2 cup, chopped
Butter 1 tablespoon

Mix together bread cubes, brown sugar, salt and cinnamon. Add remaining ingredients except butter and combine well. Pour this mixture into well-greased baking dish. Dab with butter. Bake in a preheated oven at 325° for about 40 minutes or until toothpick inserted in center of pudding comes out clean.

Instant Fruit Sherbet

Lee Schillereff—Canon City, Colorado: "I suggest using a combination of the following fruits: strawberries, blueberries, apricots, peaches, nectarines, oranges and cantaloupe."

Fresh fruit 1 pound, cut into
   1-inch cubes
Sugar 6 tablespoons
Buttermilk, milk, yogurt or low-cal
   sour cream 1 cup

Egg 1
Lemon or lime squeezed to
   make 2 tablespoons

   Place cubes of fruit on tray and freeze for 1 1/2 hours. When frozen, pour into a food processor with the remaining ingredients.Blend until smooth and creamy. Serve immediately or store in freezer. Serves 4-6.

Cascade Peaches 'n Cream Ice

Barbara Sabol—Cascade, Colorado: "With no dairy products, this is a low-fat recipe appropriate for those who don't eat eggs. Really refreshing. Remember... Colorado-grown peaches are excellent!"

Knox® gelatin 1 package
Liquid non-dairy
   coffee creamer 1/2 cup
Peaches 4 cups, diced

Sugar or substitute to taste
Almond flavoring 1/2 teaspoon,
   if desired

   Soften gelatin in liquid non-dairy creamer and set aside. Puree peaches in a blender and add sugar and almond flavoring. Heat the gelatin and creamer just until boiling. Add to peaches and blend together 2-3 minutes. Pour mixture into ice-cream maker and follow manufacturer's freezing instructions. For a "wild" topping, puree 1 cup of wild, mountain raspberries in blender and pour over the top of the chilled ice. Serves 6.

Summer Sundaes

Ice cream dressed up with a homemade, fresh-strawberry sauce.

Strawberries 2 cups, sliced
Lemon juice 1 1/2 teaspoons
Sugar 1/2 cup
Orange juice 1/3 cup

Cornstarch 4 teaspoons
Triple Sec® 2 teaspoons
Ice cream any flavor
Whipped cream as desired

In a small saucepan, bring strawberries, lemon juice and sugar to a boil over medium heat. Lower heat. Mix together the orange juice and cornstarch until cornstarch is dissolved. Stir into strawberries. Continue to simmer, stirring constantly, until thick. Remove from heat. Drizzle in Triple Sec® and stir well. Scoop ice cream into dessert dishes. Cover with strawberry sauce and top with whipped cream. For garnish, try a strawberry half, cherry or fresh mint sprig.

Waunita Banana Split Dessert

Thanks to the Waunita Hot Springs Ranch for this fun dessert--an ice-cream cake inspired by banana splits that easily serves a party of 12.

Graham cracker crumbs
  1 1/2 cups
Butter 6 tablespoons, melted
Powdered sugar 2 cups
Butter 1/2 cup

Eggs 2
Bananas 3-4
Crushed pineapple 1 (18 oz.) can
Whipped cream 4 cups
Nuts 2/3 cup, chopped

Mix together graham cracker crumbs and 6 tablespoons butter. Press this into a 9x13 pan. In mixing bowl, beat sugar, remaining butter and eggs for 10 minutes. Spread evenly over the pressed crumbs. Slice bananas and arrange on top of sugar-butter mixture. Drain pineapple in the can and spread over bananas. Spoon on whipped cream and spread until 1/2-inch thickness. Sprinkle with chopped nuts and chill well.

Cloud City Magic Coconut Pie

Judy Clemmer—Leadville Country Inn, Leadville, Colorado: "The magic is in the crust--it makes its own!"

Eggs 4
Sugar 1 3/4 cups
Flour 1/2 cup
Milk 2 cups

Butter or margarine
  1/4 cup, melted
Coconut 1 1/2 cups, flaked
Vanilla 1 teaspoon

Combine all ingredients in order and mix well. Pour into greased pie plate. Bake in a preheated oven at 350° for 45 minutes or until golden brown.

> *Leadville, also known as "Cloud City," sits amongst the Sawatch Mountains in southern Colorado and retains a colorful mining history. At 10,152 feet, the area is said to withstand 10 months of winter a year. Guests at the Leadville Country Inn make the most of the snowy winters with Victorian sleigh rides, followed by a lavish fireside feast served by Victorian-dressed waiters.*

Outrageous Rocky Mountain Pie

Butter 1/2 cup
Chocolate chips 1 cup
Graham cracker crumbs 3 cups
Cream cheese 1 package,
  room temperature
Peanut butter 3/4 cup, smooth

Sweetened condensed
  milk 1 can
Lemon juice 3 tablespoons
Vanilla 1 1/4 teaspoons
Whipped cream 1 cup
Chocolate syrup 2 teaspoons

In a medium saucepan or double boiler, melt butter and chocolate chips over low heat. Remove from heat. Stir in graham cracker crumbs until well mixed. Spoon into greased pie pan and press evenly. Refrigerate for 30 minutes or more. In large bowl, beat cream cheese. Add peanut butter and milk and continue beating until smooth. Add lemon juice and vanilla. Gently fold in whipped cream. Pour into crust and spread evenly. Drizzle on chocolate syrup. Chill until set, 4-5 hours. Keep leftovers refrigerated.

Silverton Rhubarb Crisp

Rhubarb 6 cups, diced
fresh or frozen
Lemon peel 1, grated
Sugar 2/3 cup
Brown sugar 3/4 cup, packed
Flour 3/4 cup
Butter 1/3 cup, softened
Cinnamon 1 tablespoon

Bourbon Sauce:
Egg yolks 3
Sugar 1/3 cup
Whipping cream 1 cup
Milk 1/3 cup
Salt a pinch
Bourbon 1/4 cup

Combine rhubarb, lemon peel and sugar in a two-quart casserole. Combine brown sugar, flour, butter and cinnamon and spread over rhubarb mixture. Bake in a preheated oven at 350° for one hour. For sauce: Beat egg yolks and sugar until light and lemon-colored. Whisk in cream and milk. Cook over hot, but not boiling, water until it thickens. Stir in bourbon and salt and cook five minutes. Pour over Crisp.

Silverton's Rhubarb Roots

The legend goes something like this: An Italian immigrant left his homeland with his wife and family to stake a claim in the mining industry at Silverton. In order to treat her family for sickness in the new world, his wife brought along many herbs, including rhubarb, which she planted in her home garden. The first winter was an eternity for the wife, who missed old friends and rarely saw her husband, who spent weeks at a time at the mine. She contemplated ingesting the rhubarb's poisonous leaves and end her miserable loneliness. Fortunately, she waited. Along with spring came many surprises: letters from home and Italian neighbors. Moreover, her husband found a large gold nugget, with which he bought a local store and retired from mining. To celebrate, the wife baked rhubarb pies to share with friends. And, she split her rhubarb root for friends to propagate. And that's the legend of how rhubarb, apparently a proliferate root, spread throughout San Juan County.

(Courtesy of Silverton Public Library)

Ultimate Pumpkin Pie

Tracey Schollin—Boulder, Colorado: "The first time I served this was to friends after a game of Ultimate Frisbee. After everyone devoured it, I took votes as to what to name it. The decision was unanimous."

Flour 1 1/4 cups
Baking powder 1/8 teaspoon
Salt 1/4 teaspoon
Butter 1 stick plus 1 tablespoon
Water 3 1/2 tablespoons, iced
Brown Sugar 3/4 cup
Salt 1/2 teaspoon
Cinnamon 1 teaspoon

Nutmeg a pinch
Ginger 1/2 teaspoon
Egg 1, lightly beaten
Pumpkin 1 1/2 cups, canned
Half-and-half 2/3 cup
Vanilla 1 teaspoon
Kahlua® 1/3 cup

Mix together flour, baking powder and salt. With a fork, cut in butter and work it until well-distributed. Add tablespoons of water, mixing thoroughly after each one. Dough should hold together, but be stiff. Roll it out on a floured surface, large enough to cover pie plate. Fit it evenly into plate and finish off edges. For filling: Combine brown sugar, salt and spices. Blend in egg. In separate bowl, mix together pumpkin, half-and-half and vanilla. Blend in with pumpkin mixture and add Kahlua®. Pour batter into pie crust. Bake in a preheated oven at 425° for 15 minutes; reduce oven setting to 350° and bake 30 minutes longer. Whipped cream may be spread evenly over the top of the pie before serving. Also looks nice and tastes even better garnished with pecan halves. Makes one 9-inch pie.

Flan de Juan

John Wheats—Telluride, Colorado: "The perfect ending to a massive Mexican meal."

Sugar 1 1/2 cups
Condensed milk 14-ounce can
Water 1 cup

Vanilla 1 1/4 teaspoons
Eggs 4, well beaten
Rum 2 tablespoons (optional)

Stir sugar in a heavy skillet over a low flame until it melts and turns golden. Spread evenly in casserole pan. As it cools, beat milk, 1 cup of water, vanilla and eggs. Pour over sugar. Place dish inside larger pan with 1 inch of water. Bake in a preheated oven at 350° for about 1 1/2 hours. If desired, drizzle on a little rum before serving.

Cortez Clouds

Also known as sopaipillas, these are the Mexican equivalent to donuts. Frying makes the dough get puffy. Squeeze honey into the center and sprinkle on cinnamon. Good for breakfast, or as dessert later on.

Flour 1 2/3 cups
Baking powder 2 teaspoons
Salt 1 teaspoon

Butter 2 tablespoons
Water 2/3 cup, very cold
Oil for frying

Mix together sifted flour, baking powder, salt and butter. Gradually mix in 2/3 cup of very cold water, adding just enough to hold dough together. Knead until smooth and set it aside for about 5 minutes. As dough rests, pour hot oil into frying pot and heat until very hot. Roll pastry until 1/8-inch thick. Cut into palm-sized squares and fry in oil. Turn them frequently until golden. Drain on paper towels and serve while still warm. For sweeter sopaipillas, sprinkle sifted powdered sugar over them while they are hot.

Mexican Wedding Cookies

Don't wait for a wedding to try this south-of-the-border tradition.

Butter 1 1/2 cups
Powdered sugar 3/4 cup
Vanilla 1 3/4 teaspoons
Flour 3 1/2 cups

Salt 1/2 teaspoon
Walnuts 1 1/2 cups, ground
Powdered sugar

Beat butter until fluffy. Add powdered sugar and vanilla and beat smooth. Mix in flour, salt and nuts. Allow the batter to chill for about 30 minutes. Form into one-inch balls and place on cookie sheet. Bake in a preheated oven at 325° for about 20 minutes. Do not let the cookies brown. Roll in powdered sugar immediately after removing them from the oven. Roll in powdered sugar a second time, after they have cooled.

Huckleberry Pie

If you're lucky enough to be in the Rocky Mountains in late summer, plan a hike, take along a bucket , heap it high with huckleberries and bake this pie once you're home. P.S. Blueberries may be substituted for the unfortunate folks who can't get their hands on huckleberries.

Flour 2 1/4 cups
Salt 1/4 teaspoon
Butter 3/4 cup, cold
Water 1/2 cup, ice cold
Sugar 3/4 cup

Flour 3 tablespoons
Salt dash
Huckleberries 4 1/2 cups, washed and patted dry

Sift flour and salt. Cut in butter with a fork and mix thoroughly. Add water, gradually, mixing well after each addition. Dough will become stiff; if necessary, work it with hands. Form into two balls, one slightly larger than the other, and chill for about 1/2 hour. Once chilled, roll out larger ball to line a 9-inch pie pan. Roll the smaller ball until it is big enough to cover the pie. Set both in the refrigerator until ready to use. Sprinkle sugar, flour and a dash of salt over the huckleberries and toss gently. Pour into pie shell, cover with top crust and seal sides by pinching crusts together. Tines of a fork may be used to crimp edges. Prick the top with a fork a couple of times to allow steam to release. If desired, brush top crust lightly with egg white and dust with sugar. Bake in a preheated oven at 350° for about 30 minutes. Cool about 20 minutes before serving.

Yogurt and Granola Pie

Molly Mahoney—Telluride, Colorado: "My favorite summer dessert!"

Pie crust bottom only
Evaporated milk or whipped topping 1 cup

Yogurt 2 cups, fruit flavors are best, any combination
Granola 1/2 cup

Bake in a preheated oven the pie crust and allow to cool thoroughly. Refrigerate until ready to fill. Mix together well the milk (or whipped topping) and yogurt. Pour into pie shell and freeze overnight.   Sprinkle granola evenly over top before serving.

Breakfast and Brunch

 Time to rise and shine, and prepare for a day on the slopes. Here are some hearty and light dishes... French toast, pancakes and eggs...

Islander French Toast

A favorite recipe shared by Sallie Clark, owner of the Holden House.

Potato bread 9 slices	**Sugar** 1 tablespoon
Eggs 6	**Flaked coconut** for topping
Milk 2 cups	**Bananas** 2, slice
Pineapple flavoring 1/2 teaspoon	**Butter**
Coconut flavoring 1/2 teaspoon	**Raspberry syrup**
Banana flavoring 1/2 teaspoon	**Whipped cream**
	Raspberries fresh or frozen (thawed)
	Pineapple 9 rings

Slice bread crosswise. Whip eggs, milk, flavorings and sugar. Dip bread slices in egg mixture and place on a well-greased, insulated cookie sheet. Pour any left-over egg mixture over slices and let stand for 10 minutes. Sprinkle lightly with coconut. Bake in a preheated oven at 400° for about 8 to 10 minutes. Flip each slice and sprinkle again with coconut and top with sliced bananas. Continue to bake until coconut and toast is golden. Top with butter, syrup and a dollop of whipped cream. Serve with raspberries on the side. Garnish with a pineapple ring and a sprinkle of coconut.

A romantic and comfortable Victorian bed-and-breakfast, the Holden House was built in 1902 by Isabel Holden, the widow of a wealthy Colorado Springs businessman. The inn was restored in 1985 by Sallie and Welling Clark, who've filled their Colorado Springs inn with antiques, family heirlooms and oft-returning guests. On the list of attractions to the inn... sumptuous gourmet breakfasts.

French Toast with Bacon

Cecilia Woods—Glenwood Springs, Colorado: "Serve with fresh coffee and sliced peaches. I like to use French bread for this recipe, but it's just as delicious with whole-wheat or raisin breads."

Bread 12 slices, cut diagonally
Eggs 4 large
Milk 1 cup
Vegetable oil

Powdered sugar
Maple syrup
Bacon 1 pound

Soak bread in eggs beaten with milk. Heat oil in skillet and cook bread until browned on both sides. Remove toast to warm platter and keep warm until ready to serve. Sprinkle on powdered sugar and serve with maple syrup and strips of cooked bacon.

Historically known as a freight route built to transport silver from Ashcroft to the nearest railroad, Pearl Pass is better known to mountain bikers as a two-wheeling endurance test. Leaving from Ashcroft, riders ascend more than 3,000 feet and travel eight miles before reaching the pass. From there, they choose between heading back toward Aspen or rolling 12 miles ahead to the cozy town of Crested Butte.

Pearl Pass Pancakes

Milk 1 1/2 cups
Rolled oats 3/4 cup
Oil 2 tablespoons
Eggs 2, beaten
Wheat germ 2 tablespoons

Bran 2 tablespoons
Whole wheat flour 1/2 cup
Brown sugar 2 tablespoons
Baking powder 1 teaspoon
Salt 1/4 teaspoon

Combine milk and oats and set aside for at least 5 minutes. Mix in oil and eggs. Stir in remaining ingredients just until moist. For each pancake, pour 1/4 cup of batter on hot, oiled skillet. Turn when top is bubbly, and cook the other side.

Ruffled Crepes Isabel

Sallie Clark, innkeeper and gourmet breakfast chef at the Holden House 1902—Colorado Springs: "We like to use herbs fresh from the garden." The recipe is named after the Victorian inn's original owner, Isabel Holden.

Crepes:
Flour 1 1/4 cups
Sugar 2 tablespoons
Salt a pinch
Eggs 3
Milk 1 1/2 cups
Butter 2 tablespoons, melted
Lemon extract 1 teaspoon

Egg mixture:
Eggs 7
Milk 1 cup
Salt 1/2 teaspoon
Pepper 1/4 teaspoon
Turkey bacon 6 slices
cooked and crumbled
Cheddar cheese shredded

Mix together all crepe ingredients and set aside to rest for about 5 minutes. Pour crepes onto a well-greased skillet or crepe maker to make five-inch rounds. Extras may be stored in the refrigerator. Combine all egg mixture ingredients, except bacon and cheese. Press crepes into generously greased muffin tins, lightly ruffling the edges but being careful not to tear. Place a small square of cheese in bottom of tin and carefully pour in egg mixture. Top with crumbled bacon. Bake at 375° for 15 to 20 minutes or until mixture is firm and crepes are lightly browned. Carefully loosen crepe cups from tins with a fork or knife. Garnish with a dollop of sour cream and fresh parsley, dill or tarragon.

Yet, who can help loving the land that has taught us
Six hundred and eighty-five ways to dress eggs?

—Thomas Moore

Italiano Eggs Florentine

This and the recipe below are two more favorite dishes prepared by Sallie Clark.

Pillsbury All Ready Crusts 2
Eggs 4
Milk 2 cups
Flour 4 tablespoons
Frozen spinach 1 package
Cheese 1 cup, shredded,
   jack or Swiss

Turkey bacon 8 slices,
   sliced in half
Dried basil
Marinara sauce 1 small jar
Fresh parsley

Divide each pie crust into four sections to form a ball. Roll each section out on a flowered board and place in 12-ounce quiche dishes, ruffling edges. Beat eggs, milk and flour together and set aside. Evenly divide thawed spinach and place in each quiche crust. Pour egg and milk mixture over spinach and top with shredded cheese. Lay 4 half slices of bacon slices over cheese and sprinkle with a dash of basil. Bake at 375° for 40 minutes until quiche is firm and slightly browned. Garnish each with 3 tablespoons of marinara sauce and a sprig of fresh parsley.

Holden House Eggs Fiesta

Eggs 12
Flour tortillas 3, small
Cheddar cheese 6 slices
Bacon bits or crumbled
   cooked turkey bacon

Cilantro
Sour cream for garnish
Mild picante sauce
Parsley

Spray 6 individual souffle dishes with non-stick spray. Break 2 eggs into each dish. Slice tortillas in half and place in dishes with straight edge in center and half-circle edge hanging on outer edge of dish. Top with a slice of cheese and crumbled bacon bits. Sprinkle on chopped cilantro. Bake at 375° for 30 minutes, until eggs are cooked, cheese is melted and tortilla is golden. Top with a dollop of sour cream and teaspoon of picante. Garnish with parsley.

Breakfast at Rawah Ranch

A melange of vegetables mixed with eggs and cheese, prepared by Rawah Ranch owner and breakfast gourmet--Ardy Kunz.

Flour 1 cup
Margarine 1 cup, melted
Eggs one dozen
Baking powder 2 teaspoons
Cottage cheese 2 pounds
Jack cheese 1 pound
Garlic powder 2 teaspoons
Onion powder 2 teaspoons
Salt and pepper to taste

Any of the following diced
vegetables may be added:
Sauteed mushrooms
Green pepper
Broccoli
Tomatoes
Green onions

Mix flour, margarine and other ingredients. Bake in a preheated oven in a greased 3-quart baking dish at 350° for 1 hour. Serve immediately.

Nestled in a little-known valley alongside the Laramie River in northern Colorado, Rawah Ranch was named after the 76,000 acres of stunningly beautiful wilderness area surrounding it. Operating as a dude ranch since 1950, this mountain retreat offers guests a relaxing and invigorating sabbatical from city life. The ranch is known for its exceptionally good string of horses, some of Colorado's finest fly fishing, and miles of hiking through the wilderness and National Forest.

And to top it off--there's the food. The day begins with a hearty breakfast to refuel for the day's activities. At day's end, guests wind down with a feast served family-style in the main lodge: grilled steaks, ribs and chicken, home-baked breads and decadent desserts.

Beverages

Like the gold and silver mining rush that magnetized many a hopeful millionaire to the Rockies a century ago, thousands of skiers make the pilgrimage to Colorado ski slopes each winter. And if skiing pleasure is proportional to wealth, they will ultimately find an enriching experience: 23,000 acres of skiable terrain, divvied up between 27 resorts and 250 lifts. As a tribute to the winter sport, we start off the beverage chapter with apres ski favorites... hot toddies. We suggest pulling off the ski boots, pulling up a seat fireside and sharing a couple of these with good friends.

Billy Kidd Hot Buttered Rum

Named after Steamboat Springs' skiing superstar, Billy Kidd, the 1964 Olympic silver medalist and 1970 world champion.

Dark rum 2 ounces
Cinnamon sticks 2
Ground cloves 1/2 teaspoon
Nutmeg 1/2 teaspoon

Boiling water 2 cups
Honey 2 teaspoons
Butter 1 tablespoon
Ground cinnamon dash

Into two large mugs, pour one ounce of rum. Place a cinnamon stick in each mug, and mix in the cloves and nutmeg. Pour in a cup of boiling water. Stir in honey. Float a dab of butter on each and sprinkle on a pinch of cinnamon.

Rocky Mountain Mulled Wine

Water 1 cup
Cinnamon sticks 2
Cloves 6-8
Orange rind 1, grated

Lemon rind 1, grated
Sugar 2 teaspoons
Red wine 1 bottle
Orange slices to garnish

In a large saucepan, bring water, spices, fruit rinds and sugar to a boil. Immediately stir in wine and bring back to a boil. Remove from stove and pour into mugs. Garnish with orange slices.

> *The first fall of snow is not only an event, it is a magical event. You go to bed in one kind of world and wake up in another quite different, and if this is not enchantment then where is it to be found?*
>
> *— J.B. Priestley*

Powderhound Irish Coffee

A rich relative of regular Irish coffee.

Irish whisky 2 ounces
Irish cream liqueur 2 ounces
Sugar 2 teaspoons

Coffee 2 cups, freshly brewed
Whipped cream 1/2 cup
Creme de menthe

Into two mugs, pour half the whisky, liqueur and sugar. Stir in coffee. Garnish with a dollop of whipped cream and a drizzle of creme de menthe.

Molly Brown Margaritas

Out of Colorado's colorful cast of characters steps Molly Brown. Known as a "crasher" of social circles, and something of a "tart" (like these very margaritas), Miss Brown achieved fame by surviving the sinking of the Titanic. Her life is immortalized by the Broadway musical, "The Unsinkable Molly Brown." Served in tall glasses rimmed with salt, these margaritas immortalize parties year-round.

Tequila 2/3 cup
Lime juice 2/3 cup
Limeade 2/3 cup
Sugar 3 teaspoons

Grand Marnier 1/3 cup
Ice
Coarse salt
Lime wedges

Pour tequila, lime juice, Grand Marnier, limeade and sugar into an electric blender. Blend with about four cups of ice until all ice is thoroughly crushed. Moisten four glass rims with water or lime juice and dip in coarse salt to evenly coat. Pour in frozen margaritas. Garnish with lime wedges.

Melon-Berry Swink Drinks

In 1878, George Swink inaugurated Rocky Mountain Watermelon Day. Joining in the festivities were 8,000 visitors, Governor John Routt, and a grand total of 10,000 melons. We'd like to toast the genius of Mr. Swink with these watermelon-strawberry coolers.

Strawberries 1 cup
Watermelon 2 cups
Rum 1/3 cup

Orange juice 1/4 cup
Lime juice 1/4 cup
Sugar 1 tablespoon

Hull the strawberries and place in a freezer bag. Seed watermelon and cut into one-inch chunks. Place in the plastic bag with strawberries and freeze for about five hours. Mix together remaining ingredients. In an electric blender, puree the fruit and juice mixture until smooth. Serve in tall glasses, garnished with lime or orange slices.

COLORADO FACTS & INFORMATION

Colorado is the eighth largest state in the nation and contains 75 percent of all the area in the United States over 10,000 feet. Fifty-three of Colorado's peaks are more than 14,000 feet in elevation. The state's mountainous areas are six times that of Switzerland.

Statehood: August 1, 1876; thirty-eighth state

Name Origin: Named after the Colorado River which received its name from the early Spanish explorers because of its red color.

State Capital: Denver, founded 1858

State Nickname: Centennial State

State Motto: "Nothing without Providence"

State Bird: Lark Bunting

State Animal: Rocky Mountain bighorn sheep

State Flower: Rocky Mountain columbine

State Tree: Colorado blue spruce

TRAVEL & ACCOMMODATIONS

Colorado Tourism Board
1625 Broadway, Suite 1700
Denver, CO 80202
(800) 433-2656 (vacation kit orders)

National Park Service
P.O. Box 25287
Lakewood, CO 80225
(303) 969-2000

Bed & Breakfast Rocky Mountains
P.O. Box 804
Colorado Springs, CO 80901
(800) 825-0225   (800) 733-8415   (719) 630-3433

Colorado Dude and Guest Ranch Association
P.O. Box 300
Tabernash, CO 80478

Phone Numbers for Travel and Events Information
(by region)

Northwest (800) 327-8789
Southwest (800) 933-4340
North Central (800) 444-0447
South Central (800) 637-6238
Northeast (800) 544-8609
Southeast (800) 338-6633

Index

More Cookbooks from Golden West Publishers

CHRISTMAS IN COLORADO

Recipes, traditions and folklore for the Holiday Season — or for all year long. Create a southwestern holiday spirit in *your* home with this wonderful cook book!

5 1/2 x 8 1/2—128 pages . . . $9.95

EATING INN STYLE! COLORADO COOK BOOK

Indulge your romantic mood with delicious dishes from bed and breakfast inns across Colorado. Enjoy gourmet recipes for breakfasts as well as appetizers, breads, salads, main dishes, and desserts. Create a brunch for friends or a romantic weekend getaway for two!

5 1/2 x 8 1/2—128 pages . . . $8.95

TORTILLA LOVERS COOK BOOK

From tacos to tostadas, enchiladas to nachos, every dish celebrates the tortilla! More than 70 easy to prepare, festive recipes for breakfast, lunch and dinner. Filled with Southwestern flavors! By Bruce Fischer and Bobbie Salts.

5 1/2 x 8 1/2 — 112 pages . . . $6.95

SALSA LOVERS COOK BOOK

More than 180 taste-tempting recipes for salsas that will make every meal a special event! Salsas for salads, appetizers, main dishes and desserts! Put some salsa in your life! More than 275,000 copies sold!

5 1/2 x 8 1/2—128 pages . . . $6.95

QUICK-N-EASY MEXICAN RECIPES

More than 175 favorite Mexican recipes you can prepare in less than thirty minutes. Traditional items such as tacos, tostadas and enchiladas. Also features easy recipes for salads, soups, breads, desserts and drinks.

5 1/2 x 8 1/2—128 pages . . . $6.95

ORDER BLANK

GOLDEN WEST PUBLISHERS

☼ 4113 N. Longview Ave. • Phoenix, AZ 85014

www.goldenwestpublishers.com • **1-800-658-5830** • FAX 602-279-6901

Qty	Title	Price	Amount
	Apple Lovers Cook Book	**6.95**	
	Berry Lovers Cook Book	**6.95**	
	Best Barbecue Recipes	**6.95**	
	Chili-Lovers' Cook Book	**6.95**	
	Chip and Dip Lovers Cook Book	**6.95**	
	Christmas in Colorado Cook Book	**9.95**	
	Colorado Cook Book	**6.95**	
	Cowboy Cook Book	**7.95**	
	Easy RV Recipes!	**6.95**	
	Easy Recipes for Wild Game & Fish	**6.95**	
	Eating Inn Style! Colorado Cook Book	**8.95**	
	New Mexico Cook Book	**6.95**	
	Quick-n-Easy Mexican Recipes	**6.95**	
	Recipes for a Healthy Lifestyle	**6.95**	
	Salsa Lovers Cook Book	**6.95**	
	Take This Chile and Stuff It!	**6.95**	
	Tortilla Lovers Cook Book	**6.95**	
	Veggie Lovers Cook Book	**6.95**	
	Wholly Frijoles! The Whole Bean Cook Book	**6.95**	
	Wyoming Cook Book	**6.95**	

Shipping & Handling Add: United States $4.00
Canada & Mexico $6.00—All others $13.00

☐ My Check or Money Order Enclosed

☐ MasterCard ☐ VISA

Total $ _____

(Payable in U.S. funds)

Acct. No. _____ Exp. Date _____

Signature _____

Name _____ Phone _____

Address _____

City/State/Zip _____

Call for a FREE catalog of all of our titles

5/04   This order blank may be photocopied   Colorado Ck Bk